IMISCOE Research Series

Now accepted for Scopus! Content available on the Scopus site in spring 2021. This series is the official book series of IMISCOE, the largest network of excellence on migration and diversity in the world. It comprises publications which present empirical and theoretical research on different aspects of international migration. The authors are all specialists, and the publications a rich source of information for researchers and others involved in international migration studies. The series is published under the editorial supervision of the IMISCOE Editorial Committee which includes leading scholars from all over Europe. The series, which contains more than eighty titles already, is internationally peer reviewed which ensures that the book published in this series continue to present excellent academic standards and scholarly quality. Most of the books are available open access.

More information about this series at http://www.springer.com/series/13502

Rosita Fibbi • Arnfinn H. Midtbøen
Patrick Simon

Migration and Discrimination

IMISCOE Short Reader

 Springer

Rosita Fibbi
Swiss Forum for Migration and
Population Studies
University of Neuchâtel
Neuchatel, Switzerland

Arnfinn H. Midtbøen
Institute for Social Research
Oslo, Norway

Patrick Simon
National Institute for Demographic Studies
Paris, France

ISSN 2364-4087   ISSN 2364-4095   (electronic)
IMISCOE Research Series
ISBN 978-3-030-67280-5   ISBN 978-3-030-67281-2   (eBook)
https://doi.org/10.1007/978-3-030-67281-2

This Springer imprint is published by the registered company Springer Nature Switzerland AG
The registered company address is: Gewerbestrasse 11, 6330 Cham, Switzerland

Foreword

This book reflects a growing concern in European migration studies. For decades, migration scholars have studied immigrants' access to key social domains, such as education and the labor market, as part of a broader process of integration, often implicitly assuming that later generations will overcome the barriers opposing their immigrant parents or grandparents. Today, there is ample evidence that both immigrants and their descendants – many of whom constitute what we in this book refer to as ethno-racial minority groups – face discrimination when trying to access goods or services in Europe. Efforts to measure and understand the prevalence of discrimination, as well as concerns over the consequences of such experiences, have resulted in the fast-growing field of discrimination studies.

We have been part of this development by our own research on ethnic and racial discrimination, but also by establishing a research cluster devoted to discrimination studies within the IMISCOE network. Formally established at the 2015 IMISCOE conference in Geneva, the research cluster *Discrimination in Cross-National Perspective* aimed to put this issue front-stage, emphasizing the role of discrimination in migrants' and their descendants' integration processes and in the transformation of European countries as multicultural societies. By organizing panel sessions on discrimination in the subsequent IMISCOE annual conferences, we have brought together scholars from across Europe and North America to engage in critical debates about methods, theories, results, and interpretations.

The current book is an extension of this endeavor. The book provides a state-of-the-art overview of the research on discrimination, with a particular focus on discrimination against immigrants and their descendants. Structured as a short reader available to undergraduate and graduate students, scholars, policy makers, and the general public, it covers the ways in which discrimination is defined and conceptualized, how it may be measured and theorized, and how it may be combatted by law and policy. The book also presents recent empirical results from studies on discrimination across Europe and North America to exemplify how research in this field is conducted.

This book distinguishes itself from other handbooks in several respects. It is short and concise. It focuses mostly on the labor market because of major advances in recent empirical studies in this domain, but empirical examples are also drawn from studies of discrimination in housing, health, access to social services, and more generally on the subjective experiences of being a member of discriminated groups. The reader is further rooted in an interdisciplinary approach, reflecting that discrimination is studied across the social sciences. Finally, the book has a broad European scope, mirroring the expanding research on and growing awareness of discrimination on this side of the Atlantic and reflecting the overall mission of the IMISCOE network.

We wish to thank the IMISCOE editorial committee for the invitation to write a short reader on migration and discrimination as part of the network's new short book series, and especially the head of the committee, Anna Triandafyllidou, for her inspiring encouragement. We also wish to thank our respective research institutions – the Swiss Forum for Migration and Population Studies at the University of Neuchâtel, Institute for Social Research in Oslo and INED in Paris – for allowing us to find time to work on this book and for funding travel to Oslo and Paris for joint discussions and stimulating writing sessions.

Neuchatel, Switzerland   Rosita Fibbi

Oslo, Norway   Arnfinn H. Midtbøen

Paris, France   Patrick Simon
May 2020

Contents

Chapter 1
Introduction: The Case for Discrimination Research

European societies are more ethnically diverse than ever. The increasing migration-related diversity has fostered dramatic changes since the 1950s, among them the rise of striking ethno-racial inequalities in employment, housing, health, and a range of other social domains. The sources of these enduring inequalities have been a subject of controversy for decades. To some scholars, ethno-racial gaps in such outcomes are seen as transitional bumps in the road toward integration, while others view structural racism, ethnic hostility, and subtle forms of outgroup-bias as fundamental causes of persistent ethno-racial inequalities. These ethno-racial disadvantages *can* be understood as evidence of widespread discrimination; however, scholarly debates reflect striking differences in the conceptualization and measurement of discrimination in the social sciences.

What discrimination is, as well as how and why it operates, are differently understood and studied by the various scholarships and scientific fields. A large body of research has been undertaken over the previous three decades, using a variety of methods – qualitative, quantitative, and experimental. These research efforts have improved our knowledge of the dynamics of discrimination in Europe and beyond. It is the ambition of this book to summarize how we frame, study, theorize, and aim at combatting ethno-racial discrimination in Europe.

1.1 Post-War Immigration and the Ethno-racial Diversity Turn

Even though ethnic and racial diversity has existed to some extent in Europe (through the slave trade, transnational merchants, and colonial troops), the scope of migration-related diversity reached an unprecedented level in the period following World War II. This period coincides with broader processes of decolonization and the beginning of mass migration from non-European countries, be it from former

© The Author(s) 2021

R. Fibbi et al., *Migration and Discrimination*, IMISCOE Research Series,
https://doi.org/10.1007/978-3-030-67281-2_1

colonies to the former metropoles (from the Caribbean or India and Pakistan to the UK; South-East Asia, North Africa or Sub-Saharan Africa to France) or in the context of labor migration without prior colonial ties (from Turkey to Germany or the Netherlands; Morocco to Belgium or the Netherlands, etc.).

The ethnic and racial diversity in large demographic figures began in the 1960s (Van Mol and de Valk 2016). At this time, most labor migrants were coming from other European countries, but figures of non-European migration were beginning to rise: in 1975, 8% of the population in France and the UK had a migration background, half of which originated from a non-European country. By contrast, in 2014, 9.2% of the population of the EU28 had a migration background from outside of Europe (either foreign born or native-born from foreign-born parent(s)), and this share reached almost 16% in Sweden; 14% in the Netherlands, France, and the UK; and between 10 and 13% in Germany, Belgium, and Austria. The intensification of migration, especially from Asia and Africa, has heightened the visibility of ethno-racial diversity in large European metropolises. Almost 50% of inhabitants in Amsterdam and Rotterdam have a "nonwestern *allochthon*" background (2014), 40% of Londoners are black or ethnic minorities (2011), while 30% of Berliners (2013) and 43% of Parisians (metropolitan area; 2009) have a migration background. The major facts of this demographic evolution are not only that diversity has reached a point of "super-diversity" (see Vertovec 2007; Crul 2016) in size and origins, but also that descendants of immigrants (i.e., the second generation) today make up a significant demographic group in most European countries, with the exception of Southern Europe where immigration first boomed in the 2000s.

The coming of age of the second generation has challenged the capacity of different models of integration to fulfill promises of equality, while the socio-cultural cohesion of European societies is changing and has to be revised to include ethnic and racial diversity. Native-born descendants of immigrants are socialized in the country of their parents' migration and, in most European countries, share the full citizenship of the country where they live and, consequently, the rights attached to it. However, an increasing number of studies show that even the second generation faces disadvantages in education, employment, and housing that cannot be explained by their lack of skills or social capital (Heath and Cheung 2007). The transmission of penalties from one generation to the other – and in some cases an even higher level of penalty for the second generation than for the first – cannot be explained solely by the deficiencies in human, social, and cultural capital, as could have been the case for low-skilled labor migrants arriving in the 1960s and 1970s. Indeed, the persistence of ethno-racial disadvantages among citizens who do not differ from others except for their ethnic background, their skin color, or their religious beliefs is a testament to the fact that equality for all is an ambition not yet achieved.

Citizenship status may represent a basis for differential treatment. Undoubtedly, citizenship status is generally considered a legitimate basis for differential treatment, which is therefore not acknowledged as discrimination. Indeed, in many European countries, the divide between nationals and European Union (EU) citizens lost its bearing with the extension of social rights to EU citizens (Koopmans et al. 2012). Yet, in other countries, and for non-EU citizens, foreign citizenship status creates barriers to access to social subsidies, health care, specific professions, and pensions or exposure to differential treatment in criminal justice. In most countries, voting rights are conditional to citizenship, and the movement to expand the polity to non-citizens is uneven, at least for elections of representatives at the national parliaments. Notably, in countries with restrictive access to naturalization, citizenship status may provide an effective basis for unequal treatment (Hainmueller and Hangartner 2013). The issue of discrimination among nationals, therefore, should not overshadow the enduring citizenship-based inequalities.

The gap between ethnic diversity among the population and scarcity of the representation of this diversity in the economic, political, and cultural elites demonstrate that there are obstacles to minorities entering these positions. This picture varies across countries and social domains. The UK, Belgium, or the Netherlands display a higher proportion of elected politicians with a migration background than France or Germany (Alba and Foner 2015). Some would argue that it is only a matter of time before newcomers will take their rank in the queue and access the close ring of power in one or two generations. Others conclude that there is a glass ceiling for ethno-racial minorities, which will prove as efficient as that for women to prevent them from making their way to the top. The exception that proves the rule can be found in sports, where athletes with minority backgrounds are often well represented in high-level competitions. The question is how to narrow the gap in other domains of social life, and what this gap tells us about the structures of inequalities in European societies.

1.2 Talking About Discrimination in Europe

Discrimination is as old as human society. However, the use of the concept in academic research and policy debates in Europe is fairly recent. In the case of differential treatment of ethnic and racial minorities, the concept was typically related to blatant forms of racism and antisemitism, while the more subtle forms of stigmatization, subordination, and exclusion for a long time did not receive much attention as forms of "everyday racism" (Essed 1991). The turn from explicit racism to more subtle forms of selection and preference based on ethnicity and race paved the way to current research on discrimination. In European societies, where formal equality is a fundamental principle protected by law, discrimination is rarely observed directly. Contrary to overt racism, which is explicit and easily identified, discrimination is typically a hidden part of decisions, selection processes, and choices that are not explicitly based on ethnic or racial characteristics, even though they produce unfair biases. Discrimination does not have to be intentional and it is often not even a conscious part of human action and interaction. While it is clear that discrimination exists, this form of differential treatment is hard to make visible. The major task of research in the field is thus to provide evidence of the processes and magnitude of discrimination. Beyond the variety of approaches in the different disciplines, however, discrimination researchers tend to agree on the starting point: stereotypes and prejudices are nurturing negative perceptions, more or less explicit, of individuals or groups through processes of ethnicization or racialization, which in turn create biases in decision-making processes and serve as barriers to opportunities for these individuals or groups.

Although the concepts of inequality, discrimination, and racism are sometimes used interchangeably, the concept of discrimination entails specificities in terms of social processes, power relations, and legal frameworks that have opened new perspectives to understand ethnic and racial inequalities. The genealogy of the concept and its diffusion in scientific publications still has to be studied thoroughly, and we searched in major journals to identify broad historical sequences across national contexts. Until the 1980s, the use of the concept of discrimination was not widespread in the media, public opinion, science, or policies. In scientific publications, the dissemination of the concept was already well advanced in the US at the beginning of the twentieth century in the aftermath of the abolition of slavery to describe interracial relations. In Europe, there is a sharp distinction between the UK and continental Europe in this regard. The development of studies referring explicitly to discrimination in the UK has a clear link to the post-colonial migration after World War II and the foundation of ethnic and racial studies in the 1960s. However, the references to discrimination remained quite limited in the scientific literature until the 1990s – even in specialized journals such as *Ethnic and Racial Studies*, *New Community* and its follower *Journal for Ethnic and Migration Studies*, and more recently *Ethnicities* – when the number of articles containing the term discrimination in their title or keywords increased significantly. In French-speaking journals, references to discrimination were restricted to a small number of feminist journals in the 1970s and became popular in the 1990s and 2000s in mainstream social science journals. The same held true in Germany, with a slight delay in the middle of the 2000s. Since the 2000s, the scientific publications on discrimination have reached new peaks in most European countries.

The year 2000 stands as a turning point in the development of research and public interest in discrimination in continental Europe. This date coincides with the legal recognition of discrimination by the parliament of the EU through a directive "implementing the principle of equal treatment between persons irrespective of racial or ethnic origin," more commonly called the "Race Equality Directive." This directive put ethnic and racial discrimination on the political agenda of EU countries. This political decision contributed to changing the legal framework of EU countries, which incorporated non-discrimination as a major reference and transposed most of the terms of the Race Equality Directive into their national legislation. The implementation of the directive was also a milestone in the advent of the awareness of discrimination in Europe. In order to think in terms of discrimination, there should be a principle of equal treatment applied to everyone, regardless of their ethnicity or race. This principle of equal treatment is not new, but it has remained quite formal for a long time. The Race Equality Directive represented a turning point toward a more effective and proactive approach to achieve equality and accrued sensitivity to counter discrimination wherever it takes place.

The first step to mobilize against discrimination is to launch awareness-raising campaigns to create a new consciousness of the existence of ethno-racial disadvantages. The denial of discrimination is indeed a paradoxical consequence of the extension of formal equality in post-war democratic regimes. Since racism is morally condemned and legally prohibited, it is expected that discrimination should not occur and, thus, that racism is incidental. Incidentally, an opinion survey conducted in 2000 for the European Union Monitoring Center on Racism and Xenophobia (which was replaced in 2003 by the Fundamental Rights Agency [FRA]), showed that only 31% of respondents in the EU15 at the time agreed that discrimination should be outlawed. However, the second Eurobarometer explicitly dedicated to studying discrimination in 2007 found that ethnic discrimination was perceived as the most widespread (very or fairly) type of discrimination by 64% of EU citizens (European Commission 2007). Almost 10 years later, in 2015, the answers were similar for ethnic discrimination but had increased for all other grounds except gender. Yet, there are large discrepancies between countries, with the Netherlands, Sweden, and France showing the highest levels of consciousness of ethnic discrimination (84%, 84%, and 82%, respectively), whereas awareness is much lower in Poland (31%) and Latvia (32%). In Western Europe, Germany (60%) and Austria (58%) stand out with relatively lower marks (European Commission 2015).

These Eurobarometer surveys provide useful information about the knowledge of discrimination and the attitudes of Europeans toward policies against it. However, they focus on the representation of different types of discrimination rather than the personal experience of minority members. To gather statistics on the experience of discrimination is difficult for two reasons: (1) minorities are poorly represented in surveys with relatively small samples in the general population and (2) questions about experiences of discrimination are rarely asked in non-specific surveys. Thanks to the growing interest in discrimination, more surveys are providing direct and indirect variables that are useful in studying the personal experiences of ethno-racial disadvantage.

The European Social Survey, for example, has introduced a question on perceived group discrimination (which is not exactly a personal self-reported experience of discrimination, see Chap. 4). In 2007 and 2015, the FRA conducted a specialized survey on discrimination in the 28 EU countries, the Minorities and Discrimination (EU-MIDIS) survey, to fill the gap in the knowledge of the experience of discrimination of ethnic and racial minorities. The information collected is wide ranging; however, only two minority groups were surveyed in each EU country, and the survey is not representative of the population.

Of course, European-wide surveys are not the main statistical sources on discrimination. Administrative statistics, censuses, and social surveys at the national and local levels in numerous countries bring new knowledge of discrimination, either with direct measures when this is the main topic of data collection or more indirectly when they provide information on gaps in employment or education faced by disadvantaged groups. The key point is to be able to identify the relevant population category in relation to discrimination, as we know that ethno-racial groups do not experience discrimination to the same extent. Analyses of immigrants or the second generation as a whole might miss the significant differences between – broadly speaking – European and non-European origins. Or, to put it in a different way, between white and non-white or "visible" minorities. Countries where groups with a European background make up most of the migration-related diversity typically show low levels of discrimination, while countries with high proportions of groups with non-European backgrounds, especially Africans (North and Sub-Saharan), Caribbean people, and South Asians, record dramatic levels of discrimination.

1.3 Who Is Discriminated Against? The Problem with Statistics on Ethnicity and Race

Collecting data on discrimination raises the problem of the identification of minority groups. Migration-related diversity has been designed from the beginning of mass migration based on place of birth of the individuals (foreign born) or their citizenship (foreigners). In countries where citizenship acquisition is limited, citizenship or nationality draws the boundary between "us" and "the others" over generations. This is not the case in countries with more open citizenship regimes where native-born children of immigrants acquire by law the nationality of their country of residence and thus cannot be identified by these variables. If most European countries collect data on foreigners and immigrants, a limited number identify the second generation (i.e., the children of immigrants born in the country of immigration). The question is whether the categories of immigrants and the second generation really reflect the population groups exposed to ethno-racial discrimination. As the grounds of discrimination make clear, nationality or country of birth is not the only characteristic generating biases and disadvantages: ethnicity, race, or color are directly involved. However, if it seems straightforward to define country of birth and citizenship, collecting data on ethnicity, race, or color is complex and, in Europe, highly sensitive.

Indeed, the controversial point is defining population groups by using the same characteristics by which they are discriminated against. This raises ethical, political, legal, and methodological issues. Ethical because the choice to re-use the very categories that convey stereotypes and prejudices at the heart of discrimination entails significant consequences. Political because European countries have adopted a color-blind strategy since 1945, meaning that their political philosophies consider that racial terminologies are producing racism by themselves and should be strictly avoided (depending on the countries, ethnicities receive the same blame). Legal because most European countries interpret the provisions of the European directive on data protection and their transposition in national laws as a legal prohibition. Methodological because there is no standardized format to collect personal information on ethnicity or race and there are several methodological pitfalls commented in the scientific literature. Data on ethnicity per se are collected in censuses to describe national minorities in Eastern Europe, the UK, and Ireland, which are the only Western European countries to produce statistics by ethno-racial categories (Simon 2012). The information is collected by self-identification either with an open question about one's ethnicity or by ticking a box (or several in the case of multiple choices) in a list of categories. None of these questions explicitly mention race: for example, the categories in the UK census refer to "White," "black British," or "Asian British" among other items, but the question itself is called the "ethnic group question."

In the rest of Europe, place of birth and nationality of the parents would be used as proxies for ethnicity in a limited number of countries: Scandinavia, the Netherlands, and Belgium to name a few. Data on second generations can be found in France, Germany, and Switzerland among others in specialized surveys with limitations in size and scope. Moreover, the succession of generations since the arrival of the first migrants will fade groups into invisibility by the third generation. This process is already well advanced in the oldest immigration countries, such as France, Germany, Switzerland, and the Netherlands. Asking questions about the grandparents and the previous generations is not an option since it would require hard decisions to classify those with mixed ancestry (how many ancestors are needed to belong to one category?), not to mention the problems in memory to retrieve all valuable information about the grandparents. This is one of the reasons why traditional immigration countries (USA, Canada, Australia) collect data on ethnicity through self-identification questions.

The discrepancies between official categories and those exposed to discrimination have fostered debates between state members and International Human Rights Organizations – such as the UN Committee for the Elimination of Racial Discrimination (CERD), European Commission against Racism and Intolerance (ECRI) at the Council of Europe, and the EU FRA – which claim that more data are needed on racism and discrimination categorized by ethnicity. The same applies to academia and antiracist NGOs where debates host advocates and opponents to "ethnic statistics." There is no easy solution, but the accuracy of data for the measurement of discrimination is a strategic issue for both research and policies.

1.4   Discrimination and Integration: Commonalities and Contradictions

How does research on discrimination relate to the broader field of research on immigrant assimilation or integration? On one hand, assimilation/integration and discrimination are closely related both in theory and in empirical studies. Discrimination hinders full participation in society, and the persistence of ethnic penalties across generations contradicts long-term assimilation prospects. On the other hand, both assimilation and integration theory tend to assume that the role of discrimination in shaping access to opportunities will decrease over time. Assimilation is often defined as "the decline of ethnic distinction and its corollary cultural and social difference" (Alba and Nee 2003, 11), a definition that bears an expectation that migrants and their descendants will over time cease to be viewed as different from the "mainstream population," reach parity in socioeconomic outcomes, and gradually become "one of us." In the canonical definition, integration departs from assimilation by considering incorporation as a two-way process. Migrants and ethnic minorities are expected to become full members of a society by adopting core values, norms, and basic cultural codes (e.g., language) from mainstream society, while mainstream society is transformed in return by the participation of migrants and ethnic minorities (Alba et al. 2012). The main idea is that convergence rather than differentiation should occur to reach social cohesion, and mastering the cultural codes of mainstream society will alleviate the barriers to resource access, such as education, employment, housing, and rights.

Of course, studies of assimilation and integration do not necessarily ignore that migrants and ethnic minorities face penalties in the course of the process of acculturation and incorporation into mainstream society. In the landmark book, *Assimilation in American Life*, Milton Gordon clearly spelled out that the elimination of prejudice and discrimination is a key parameter for assimilation to occur; or to use his own terms, that "attitude receptional" and "behavioral receptional" dimensions of assimilation are crucial to complete the process (Gordon 1964, 81). Yet, ethnic penalties are believed to be mainly determined by human capital and class differences and therefore progressively offset as education level rises, elevating the newcomers to conditions of the natives and reducing the social distance between groups. Stressing the importance of generational progress, assimilation theory thus tends to consider discrimination as merely a short-run phenomenon.

The main blind spots in assimilation and integration theories revolve around two issues: the specific inequalities related to the ethnicization or racialization of non-white minorities and the balance between the responsibilities of the structures of mainstream society and the agencies of migrants and ethnic minorities in the process of incorporation. Along these two dimensions, discrimination research offers a different perspective than what is regularly employed in studies of assimilation and integration.

Discrimination research tends to identify the unfavorable and unfair treatment of individuals or groups based on categorical characteristics and often shows these unfair treatments lie in the activation of stereotypes and prejudices by gatekeepers and the lack of neutrality in processes of selection. In this perspective, what has to be transformed and adapted to change the situation are the structures – the institutions, procedures, bureaucratic routines, etc. – of mainstream society, opening it up to ethnic and racial diversity to enable migrants and ethnic minorities to participate on equal footing with other individuals, independent of their identities. By contrast, in studies of assimilation and integration, explanations of disadvantages are often linked to the lack of human capital and social networks among migrants and ethnic minorities, suggesting that they have to transform themselves to be able to take full part in society. To simplify matters, studies of assimilation and integration often explain persistent disadvantages by pointing to characteristics of migrants and ethnic minorities, while discrimination research explains disadvantages by characteristics of the social and political system.

Both assimilation and integration theories have gradually opened up for including processes of ethnicization and racialization and the consequences of such processes on assimilation prospects. Most prominently, segmented assimilation theory (Portes and Rumbaut 2001; Portes and Zhou 1993) shifts the focus away from migrants' adaptation efforts and to the forms of interaction between minority groups – and prominently the second and later generations – and the receiving society. In this variant of assimilation theory, societies are viewed as structurally stratified by class, gender, and race, which powerfully influence the resources and opportunities available to immigrants and their descendants and contribute to shaping alternative paths of incorporation. According to segmented assimilation theory, children of immigrants may end up "ascending into the ranks of a prosperous middle class or join in large numbers the ranks of a racialized, permanently impoverished population at the bottom of society" (Portes et al. 2005, 1004), the latter outcome echoing worries over persistent ethnic and racial disadvantage. Another possible outcome is upward bicultural mobility (selective acculturation) of the children of poorly educated parents, protected by strong community ties.

The major question arising from these related fields of research – the literature on assimilation and integration, on the one hand, and the literature on discrimination, on the other – is whether the gradual diversification of Europe will result in "mainstream expansion," in which migrants and their descendants over time will ascend the ladders into the middle and upper classes of the societies they live in, or whether we are witnessing the formation of a permanent underclass along ethnic and racial lines. This book will not provide the ultimate answer to this question. However, by introducing the main concepts, theories, and methods in the field of discrimination, as well as pointing out key research findings, policies that are enacted to combat discrimination, and avenues for future research, we hope to provide the reader with an overview of the field.

1.5   The Content of the Book

The literature on discrimination is flourishing, and it involves a wide range of concepts, theories, methods, and findings. Chapter 2 provides the key concepts in the field. The chapter distinguishes between direct and indirect discrimination as legal and sociological concepts, between systemic and institutional discrimination, and between discrimination as intentional actions, subtle biases, and what might be referred to as the cumulative effects of past discrimination on the present. Chapter 3 reviews the main theoretical explanations of discrimination from a cross-disciplinary perspective. Mirroring the historical development of the field, it presents and discusses theories seeking the cause of prejudice and discrimination at the individual, organizational, and structural levels.

Of course, our knowledge of discrimination depends on the methods of measurement, since the phenomenon is mainly visible through its quantification. Hence, Chapter 4 offers an overview of the strengths and weaknesses of available methods of measurement, including statistical analysis of administrative data, surveys among potential victims and perpetrators, qualitative in-depth studies, legal cases, and experimental approaches to the study of discrimination (including survey experiments, lab experiments, and field experiments).

Importantly, discrimination does not occur similarly in all domains of social life, and it takes different forms according to the domain in question (e.g., the labor market, education, housing, health services, and public services). Chapter 5 taps into the large body of empirical work that can be grouped under the heading "discrimination research" in order to provide some key findings, while simultaneously highlighting a distinction between systems of differentiation and systems of equality.

What happens when discrimination occurs? Chapter 6 addresses the consequences of unfair treatment for targeted individuals and groups, as well as their reaction to it. These individual and collective responses to discrimination are seconded by policies designed to tackle discrimination. However, antidiscrimination policies vary greatly across countries, and Chapter 7 provides an overview of the different types of policies against discrimination in Europe and beyond, both public policies and schemes implemented by organizations. The chapter also reflects on some of the key political and societal debates about the implementation and the future of these policies. Chapter 8 concludes on the future of discrimination research in Europe, stressing the main challenges ahead for a burgeoning scientific field.

References

Alba, R., & Foner, N. (2015). *Strangers no more: Immigration and the challenges of integration in North America and Western Europe*. Princeton: Princeton University Press.

Alba, R., & Nee, V. (2003). *Remaking the American mainstream: Assimilation and contemporary immigration*. Cambridge: Harvard University Press.

Alba, R., Reitz, J. G., & Simon, P. (2012). National Conceptions of assimilation, integration, and cohesion. In M. Crul & J. H. Mollenkopf (Eds.), *The changing face of world cities: Young adult children of immigrants in Europe and the United States* (pp. 44–61). New York: Russel Sage.

Crul, M. (2016). Super-diversity vs. assimilation: How complex diversity in majority–minority cities challenges the assumptions of assimilation. *Journal of Ethnic and Migration Studies, 42*(1), 54–68. https://doi.org/10.1080/1369183X.2015.1061425.

Essed, P. (1991). *Understanding everyday racism: An interdisciplinary theory*. Newbury Park: Sage.

European Commission. (2007). *Discrimination in the European Union* (Special Eurobarometer, Vol. 263). Brussels: European Commission.

European Commission. (2015). *Discrimination in the EU in 2015* (Special Eurobarometer, Vol. 437). Brussels: European Commission.

Gordon, M. (1964). *Assimilation in American life: The role of race, religion, and National Origins*. New York: Oxford University Press.

Hainmueller, J., & Hangartner, D. (2013). Who gets a swiss passport? A natural experiment in immigrant discrimination. *American Political Science Review, 107*(01), 159–187. https://doi.org/10.1017/S0003055412000494.

Heath, A. F., & Cheung, S. Y. (Eds.). (2007). *Unequal chances: Ethnic minorities in Western labour markets*. Oxford: British Academy/Oxford University Press.

Koopmans, R., Michalowski, I., & Waibel, S. (2012). Citizenship rights for immigrants. National political processes and cross-national convergence in Western Europe, 1980–2008. *American Journal of Sociology, 117*(4), 1202–2045. https://doi.org/10.1086/662707.

Portes, A., & Rumbaut, R. (Eds.). (2001). *Legacies: The story of the immigrant second generation*. Los Angeles: University of California Press.

Portes, A., & Zhou, M. (1993). The new second generation: Segmented assimilation and its variants. *The Annals of the American Academy of Political and Social Science, 530*, 74–96. https://doi.org/10.1177/0002716293530001006.

Portes, A., Fernández-Kelly, P., & Haller, W. (2005). Segmented assimilation on the ground: The new second generation in early adulthood. *Ethnic and Racial Studies, 28*(6), 1000–1040. https://doi.org/10.1080/01419870500224117.

Simon, P. (2012). Collecting ethnic statistics in Europe: A review. *Ethnic and Racial Studies, 35*(8), 1366–1391. https://doi.org/10.1080/01419870.2011.607507.

Van Mol, C., & de Valk, H. (2016). Migration and immigrants in Europe: A historical and demographic perspective. In B. Garcés-Mascareñas & R. Penninx (Eds.), *Integration processes and policies in Europe* (IMISCOE Research Series). Cham: Springer.

Vertovec, S. (2007). Super-diversity and its implications. *Ethnic and Racial Studies, 30*(6), 1024–1054. https://doi.org/10.1080/01419870701599465.

Chapter 2
Concepts of Discrimination

The principle of equality constitutes the core of contemporary societies. Equality in dignity and rights provides the foundation of the Universal Declaration of Human Rights from 1948, and the right to equal treatment is the basis of the antidiscrimination acts that started spreading from the US and the UK in the mid-1960s onwards. Indeed, equality and discrimination are inherently connected: As legal scholar Sandra Fredman has pointed out (2011, 4), "classical and medieval societies were not founded on a principle of equality," and in these societies, there was no expectation of equal opportunities. Of course, this was, in practice, not the case in the early phases of modern societies either. For centuries, many groups – women, slaves, and racial and religious minorities – were excluded from the liberal rights that white men enjoyed. However, when the principle of equality was expanded to all groups and coupled with the prohibition of slavery and unequal treatment, women and various minority groups were formally granted the full scope of rights – including the right to not experience discrimination. Today, as legal scholar Tarunabh Khaitan (2015, 3–4) has suggested, "a system of law regulating discrimination has become key to how states define themselves." Of course, granting members of society formal equality of opportunity does not in itself eliminate inequalities, which have many roots. However, within the framework of formal equality, what role discrimination plays in shaping inequality becomes a major question.

Despite the fact that equality of opportunity is a core feature of contemporary societies, the concept of discrimination remains multifaceted. In the most straightforward definition, discrimination is the unequal treatment of similar individuals placed in the same situation but who differ by one or several characteristics, such as race, ethnicity, gender, (dis)ability, sexual orientation, or other categorical statuses. Discrimination may result from an explicit reservation or exclusion based on some of these characteristics or be the outcome of seemingly neutral rules or procedures that disproportionally disadvantage certain individuals or groups compared to others. These disadvantages might spur from organizational or societal cultures that favor some groups over others due to historical legacies, laws, or public policies. In earlier phases of many modern societies, discrimination was grounded in

R. Fibbi et al., *Migration and Discrimination*, IMISCOE Research Series,
https://doi.org/10.1007/978-3-030-67281-2_2

institutionalized ethnic and/or racial segregation, which prevented minority groups from applying for certain jobs or residing in specific areas (Anderson 2010). Such legally discriminatory systems were abolished mainly in the 1960s and 1970s. Yet, more subtle forms of exclusion in the educational system, labor market, criminal justice system, and public spaces remain the reality for many racialized groups today (Pager and Shepherd 2008; Reskin 2012).

These different forms of discrimination share two common features. First, discrimination is a matter of comparison: For discrimination to take place, the discriminated individual or group must be treated unfavorably compared to some other individual or group. Second, the basis for the unequal treatment is ascribed membership in a certain category that cannot be readily chosen or changed (whether the ascription reflects the actual identity if the individual is not important). Race, color, ethnic origin, and national descent constitute the grounds of what we here define as ethnic and racial discrimination. These categories are part of broader systems of status inequality, which help constitute the uneven distribution of wealth, power, and resources in society (Ridgeway 2014). As discrimination often occurs in processes of allocation of goods and positions – such as housing or employment – discrimination is fundamentally a matter of access to opportunities, power, and resources.

This chapter gives an overview of some of the key concepts in the field. It starts by distinguishing between direct and indirect discrimination in legal definitions. Next, we define the interrelated concepts of multiple discrimination and intersectionality, which increasingly are used in both legal studies and the social sciences, before giving an account of the interrelated concepts of organizational, institutional, and systemic discrimination. The chapter ends by reflecting on the complex relationship between discrimination and the endurance of categorical inequalities in societies where all members formally enjoy the principle of equality.

2.1   Direct and Indirect Discrimination

Direct discrimination is equivalent to the straightforward definition of discrimination. Ethnic or racial discrimination, according to the International Convention on the Elimination of All Forms of Racial Discrimination from 1965 (The CERD convention), takes place when individuals or groups are treated unequally because of their race, color, descent, or national or ethnic origin. However, "equal treatment may well lead to unequal results," as Fredman (2011, 177) points out. Indirect discrimination, therefore, refers to situations where seemingly neutral rules, provisions of procedures in practice produce disproportionate disadvantages for one category of individuals or groups compared to others. These two basic concepts – direct and indirect discrimination – constitute the main definitions in antidiscrimination laws in the EU, and they are equivalent to the concepts of disparate treatment and disparate impact discrimination, which are more frequently used terms in the US (Khaitan 2015).

Two important directives at the EU level protect individuals against direct and indirect discrimination: The Race Equality Directive and The Employment Equality Framework Directive (see also Chaps. 1 and 6). The predominant conception of antidiscrimination, which serves as the basis of both the two EU directives, defines as discrimination both actions, procedures, and provisions that have the purpose of unequal treatment and those that have differential treatment as an effect. This is important because it distinguishes discrimination from related concepts, such as prejudice, stereotypes, and unconscious forms of bias. To be sure, and as we will return to in the next chapter, discrimination can be caused by prejudice, stereotypes, or implicit bias. However, discrimination is not an ideology, belief, sentiment, or bias. It is a form of behavior, procedure, or policy that directly or indirectly disadvantages members of certain categories compared to others, simply because they happen to be members of that category (Fiske 1998). Consequently, defining an action as discriminatory does not require any underlying intention or motivation (Khaitan 2015). The concept of indirect discrimination makes this point particularly clear: By acknowledging that disadvantages may be produced or reinforced even by neutral rules and procedures, attention is drawn to the fact that unjustified categorical inequalities might occur independently of the intentions of individuals.

2.2 Multiple Discrimination and Intersectionality

In antidiscrimination law, as well as in theoretical and empirical discrimination research, concepts often refer to a specific ground of discrimination, such as "ethnic and racial discrimination," "gender discrimination," or "age discrimination." In recent years, however, increasing attention has been directed to the fact that discrimination may be based on multiple grounds. Black women, for example, may experience discrimination on the basis of both their racial appearance and gender. Similarly, gay Muslim men may experience discrimination based on their sexual orientation and religious background. Often, it might be hard to disentangle the various components of the differential treatment from each other. Such combinations of dimensions of difference are referred to as multiple discrimination or intersectionality (Khaitan 2015, 137). Importantly, dimensions of categorical differences – such as gender, ethnicity, race, religion, disability, sexuality, and age – can work together in ways that reinforce, multiply, or neutralize each other, depending on the context.

According to sociologist Patricia Hill Collins (2015, 2), the term intersectionality "references the critical insight that race, class, gender, sexuality, ethnicity, nation, ability, and age operate not as unitary, mutually exclusive entities, but as reciprocally constructing phenomena that in turn shape complex social inequalities." Originating from critical race theory, which criticized traditional feminism and the women's struggle for being concerned with the lives of white women and the civil rights movement for being predominantly represented by and concerned with the situation of African American men (cf., Crenshaw 1989), the term intersectionality has spread globally. Today, intersectionality may refer to a field of study, an analytical strategy that provides new perspectives on social phenomena, and as critical practices that inform social movements (Collins 2015). The concept has also had an important impact on antidiscrimination law in the sense that in the 2000s, in many countries, various grounds of discrimination have been gathered in comprehensive laws, replacing previous laws, which targeted singular grounds (Krizsan et al. 2012). In law, however, the term used is often multiple discrimination rather than intersectionality, yet some legal scholars also refer to intersectional discrimination (e.g., Fredman 2011, 140).

The term intersectionality was originally coined by the American lawyer, civil rights advocate and philosopher Kimberlé Williams Crenshaw in the article "Demarginalizing the Intersection of Race and Sex. A Black Feminist Critique of Antidiscrimination Doctrine, Feminist Theory and Antiracist Politics", published in *University of Chicago Legal Forum* in 1989. In this article, Crenshaw articulates the ideas of Black feminism as a critique of both the (male-dominated) civil rights movement and the (white female-dominated) women's movement. According to Crenshaw, both of these movements tended to marginalize black women, who experienced the multiple burdens of both racial and gender subordination. Crenshaw's ideas has influenced the development of antidiscrimination policy and laws in the US and the EU, it has inspired antiracist and feminist social movements across the globe, and it has been an important benchmark for the further theorizing of intersectionality in the humanities and the social sciences, not least in the important work of scholars such as Patricia Hill Collins and Leslie McCall.

2.3 Organizational, Institutional, and Systemic Discrimination

These key concepts of discrimination – direct, indirect, and multiple – are often used somewhat differently by legal scholars and social scientists, partly because they use the concepts for different purposes. The former needs precise and exhaustive definitions to be able to clarify whether single cases are discriminatory or not. The latter are more interested in broader patterns of group disadvantage and the role discrimination plays in creating such disadvantages. Social scientists are typically also more interested in subtle forms of exclusion that occurs in everyday interaction, as well as in the historical accumulation of group disadvantage. For these reasons, social science literature often entails broader conceptualizations of discrimination than are typically found in legal textbooks.

Since Gordon Allport published his seminal book *The Nature of Prejudice* (1954), social psychologists have argued that the formation of "in-group loyalty" often leads to "out-group rejection" and ultimately to discrimination. As will be detailed in Chap. 3, this basic insight is often applied to the workplace context, in which processes of exclusion may occur as members of privileged groups favor co-members of the same group, while "out-groups" systematically receive fewer opportunities in terms of training and development, promotions, and work assignments. Such in-group favoritism, in which people give advantages to individuals similar to themselves, is often referred to as homosocial reproduction (Kanter 1977; see also Chap. 3).

Organizational cultures may also shape patterns of interaction that over time exclude non-dominant groups. For example, in an extensive study of employment and housing discrimination suit files in the state of Ohio, Vincent Roscigno and colleagues (Roscigno 2007, 10) argue that discrimination involves much more than direct exclusion, "it also entails differential treatment once employed or once housed, where the outcome is status hierarchy maintenance." Focusing on "in-group favoritism" and not simply instances of differential treatment at the point of initial hiring implies that the structures of advantage within organizations also must be taken into account when considering the dynamics of contemporary discrimination.

Compared to direct differential treatment at the individual level, these forms of "systemic" discrimination are harder to prohibit by legislation, which normally protects individuals from differential treatment by providing the right to complain to a legal body when discrimination is perceived to have occurred. Due to the limits of prohibitions, these complaint-based models of antidiscrimination legislation have been supplemented by proactive obligations to promote equality in many European countries, as well as in North America. We will return to this development in Chap. 7. For now, it suffices to say that the introduction of proactive means implies, as the legal scholar Ronald Craig (Craig 2007, 175) has put it, a shift in focus "from the compensation of individuals for unlawful discrimination to the transformation of organizational policy, practice, and culture at the workplace."

Because proactive measures are intended to change organizational culture and not simply the behavior of single, discriminatory individuals, they are also more controversial. As pointed out in a classic text by sociologist Robert Merton (1971), social problems that are direct products of deviant behavior are easy to fight because they stand in conflict with the existing organization of society. Social problems that are by-products of social organization, by contrast, tend to remain latent due to the "normative force of the actual" (Merton 1971, 816). Reducing systemic discrimination requires a critical evaluation of organizational and administrative structures and implies that the problem might be the everyday policies of the organization itself. This represents a major challenge for antidiscrimination legislation because it presupposes a shift – psychologically and politically – which acknowledges that discrimination may be deeply entrenched in everyday practices and existing organizational cultures. Clearly, it requires a strong will to change such cultural practices to control biases in, for example, processes of selection, allocation of goods, and delivery of public services.

Importantly, these forms of organizational or systemic discrimination are not exclusive to the labor market but may apply to all kinds of institutional settings – schools, public apparatuses, housing, and criminal justice systems – as well as to the society at large. Thus, concepts such as "institutional discrimination" and "structural discrimination" are frequently used to capture the same types of phenomena. These terms are often used somewhat loosely in the literature and there are few guidelines in making clear distinctions between the concepts. A useful way of pinpointing the key content of these concepts, however, is to say that they "refer to the range of policies and practices that contribute to the systematic disadvantage of members of certain groups" (Pager and Shepherd 2008, 197; see also Chap. 3).

Particularly in the context of American race relations, structural, systemic, or institutional discrimination are often used interchangeably with the concept of institutional racism. Ward and Rivera (2014) define institutional racism as "a self-perpetuating and opaque process where, either intentionally or unintentionally, barriers and procedures which disadvantage ethnic minority groups are supported and maintained." Indeed, members of minority groups may be disadvantaged not only because of differential treatment at the individual level, but because they are part of broader societal structures that over time has come to privilege some groups over others. Present-day disadvantages that are products of discrimination in the past – for example, when children of disadvantaged parents face constrained opportunities due to historical discrimination and segregation but without necessarily being the subject of direct discrimination themselves – is often referred to as cumulative discrimination (Blank et al. 2004) or *über* discrimination (Reskin 2012) in the literature. The idea behind these concepts is to point out the potential feedback effects by which patterns of disadvantage are transferred across time, domains, and generations.

2.4 Discrimination and Inequality

The notions of cumulative disadvantage and *über* discrimination highlight the difficult relationship between racial and ethnic inequalities in society, on the one hand, and racial and ethnic discrimination, on the other. From a systems perspective, many racial and ethnic disparities in residential patterns, education, work, and health reflect deep-seated disadvantages that are due to different forms of discrimination, past and present (Anderson 2010; Pager and Shepherd 2008). In the realm of law, affirmative action has in some places been installed as a legal measure to compensate for such historical (and sometimes continuous) forms of structural discrimination, for example in the US (slavery and Jim Crow segregation), India (the caste system), and in South Africa (Apartheid) (Khaitan 2015; see also Chap. 7). In the social sciences, however, scholars are mostly concerned with distinguishing non-discriminatory factors that contribute to racial and ethnic disparities (e.g., group differences in human capital and access to social networks) from discrimination in access to opportunities. These scholarly efforts, which are obviously important in disentangling discrimination from legitimate bases of differentiation in access to resources, are nonetheless focusing exclusively on the individual level and may thus contribute to conceal more complex processes of discrimination that shape broader patterns of inequality.

However, it is not evident whether and how the effects of discrimination may cumulate over time, not least because traditional research designs measuring discrimination at one point in time and in single domains are not able to grasp the ways in which race and ethnicity may affect access to opportunity even in the absence of differential treatment (Reskin 2012). Furthermore, countries differ enormously in their historical legacies when it comes to experiences of slavery and colonialism, which arguably offer the strongest cases of historical discrimination. The US does in some respects constitute an "outlier" in discrimination research due to its history of slavery and, later on, the Jim Crow system of racial segregation and discrimination. Yet many European countries' pasts as colonial powers may clearly also affect current discourses and ethnic relations, as discussed in Chap. 1. How national histories affect the actual level of present discrimination have only recently been addressed by empirical research (Quillian et al. 2019). Suffice to say, this topic warrants more research: Whether and how racial and ethnic inequalities are reproduced across generations, and what role discrimination plays in this process, constitute a major concern in Europe today.

2.5   Conclusion

In the most straightforward sense, discrimination is defined as the unequal treatment of otherwise similar individuals due to their ascribed membership in a disadvantaged category or group. Partly as a response to a marked decrease in the most blatant forms of racism and discrimination, explicitly excluding minorities from access to housing and jobs, much attention today – in both research and law – focuses on the more subtle, indirect and covert forms of discrimination, and the extent to which discrimination contributes to prevailing racial and ethnic inequalities in societies at large. This is of crucial importance as discrimination continues to shape the access to power and resources for members of disadvantaged groups, as well as their everyday experiences and identity constructions. However, the change in focus also opens up a conceptual landscape that is more complex, more difficult to legislate and harder to enforce in practice. On top of this complexity comes the difficulties in identifying discrimination when it occurs, measuring its prevalence, and assessing its remedies and consequences. The next chapters delve into these important issues.

References

Allport, G. (1954). *The nature of prejudice*. Cambridge, MA: Addison-Wesley.
Anderson, E. (2010). *The imperative of integration*. Princeton: Princeton University Press.

Blank, R. M., Dabady, M., & Citro, C. F. (Eds.). (2004). *Measuring racial discrimination. Panel on methods for assessing discrimination.* Washington, DC: National Research Council, National Academies Press.

Collins, P. H. (2015). Intersectionality's definitional dilemmas. *Annual Review of Sociology, 41,* 1–20. https://doi.org/10.1146/annurev-soc-073014-112142.

Craig, R. (2007). *Systemic discrimination in employment and the promotion of ethnic equality.* Leiden: Martinus Nijhoff Publishers.

Crenshaw, K. (1989). Demarginalizing the intersection of race and sex. A black feminist critique of antidiscrimination doctrine, feminist theory, and antiracist politics. In *Feminism and the law: Theory, practice, and criticism.* Chicago: University of Chicago Legal Forum.

Fiske, S. (1998). Stereotyping, prejudice, and discrimination. In D. Gilbert, S. Fiske, & G. Lindzey (Eds.), *The handbook of Social psychology* (pp. 357–411). New York: McGraw Hill.

Fredman, S. (2011). *Discrimination law* (2nd ed.). Oxford: Oxford University Press.

Kanter, R. M. (1977). *Men and women of the corporation.* New York: Basic Books.

Khaitan, T. (2015). *A heory of discrimination law.* Oxford: Oxford University Press.

Krizsan, A. (2012). In H. Skjeie & J. Squires (Eds.), *Institutionalizing intersectionality: The changing nature of European equality regimes.* Basingstoke: Palgrave Macmillan.

Merton, R. (1971). Epilogue: Social problems and sociological theory. In R. Merton & R. Nisbet (Eds.), *Contemporary social problems* (pp. 793–845). New York: Harcourt Brace Jovanovich.

Pager, D., & Shepherd, H. (2008). The sociology of discrimination: Racial discrimination in employment, housing, credit, and consumer markets. *Annual Review of Sociology, 34,* 181–209. https://doi.org/10.1146/annurev.soc.33.040406.131740.

Quillian, L., Heath, A., Pager, D., Midtbøen, A. H., Fleischmann, F., & Hexel, O. (2019). Do some countries discriminate more than others? Evidence from 97 field experiments of racial discrimination in hiring. *Sociological Science, 6,* 467–496. https://doi.org/10.15195/v6.a18.

Reskin, B. F. (2012). The race discrimination system. *Annual Review of Sociology, 38,* 17–35. https://doi.org/10.1146/annurev-soc-071811-145508.

Ridgeway, C. L. (2014). Why status matters for inequality. *American Sociological Review, 79*(1), 1–16. https://doi.org/10.1177/0003122413515997.

Roscigno, V. J. (2007). *The face of discrimination: How race and gender impact work and home lives.* New York: Rowman & Littlefield Publishers.

Ward, J. D., & Rivera, M. A. (2014). *Institutional racism, organizations & public policy.* New York: Peter Lang.

Chapter 3
Theories of Discrimination

This chapter reviews the main theories developed to explain discrimination. Mirroring the historical development of the field, while reflecting a theoretically systematic approach (Pager and Shepherd 2008; Reskin 2003), the chapter adopts an approach by analytical scales to present and discuss theories of discrimination. The first section presents theories seeking the cause of prejudice and discrimination at the individual level, the second section focuses on organizational mechanisms and the third on structural determinants.

3.1 Individual-Level Theories

Defined as a behavior or a decision based on ascriptive characteristics such as race or ethnic background, discrimination differs from stereotypes and prejudices, which are mental representations summarizing the evaluation of groups. Stereotypes represent the *cognitive* component of such mental representations or attitudes, while prejudices describe the *affective* component at the roots of a biased behavior disadvantaging individuals based on their group membership or minority position. In the words of Gordon Allport, a stereotype is "an antipathy based on faulty and inflexible generalization. It may be felt or expressed. It may be directed toward a group as a whole or toward an individual because he is a member of that group" (1954, 9). Yet, attitudes are at the core of individual-level explanations of *why* discrimination occurs. As such, they are prominently discussed in this first section.

© The Author(s) 2021
R. Fibbi et al., *Migration and Discrimination*, IMISCOE Research Series,
https://doi.org/10.1007/978-3-030-67281-2_3

3.1.1   Individual Psychological Conflicts

Early theories located the motives for discrimination in the character and personality of individuals (Fiske 1998). In this perspective, internal motivations of actors are seen as rooted in individual psychological conflicts and in intrapsychic factors, such as negative attitudes against minority groups. Adorno's theory of the authoritarian personality (Adorno et al. 1950) is iconic for highlighting intrapsychic factors as causes of blatant discrimination. Echoing Freud's psychoanalysis, this theory argues that individuals inclined to conservatism, nationalism, and fascism tend to develop a rigid personality, think in rigid categories, express conventional beliefs, and often identify with and submit themselves to authority figures. According to Adorno, individuals with authoritarian personalities develop aversion toward differences to their own values and norms and thus express an overt negative attitude toward minority groups.

Though very prominent in the 1950s, the authoritarian personality theory, in its original form, is today considered outdated, notably because it fails to account for observed changes in prejudice and discrimination over time. However, in the field of political psychology, there has recently been a renewed interest in this theory (Funke et al. 2016). The association between authoritarianism and prejudice indeed seems to be driven by collective rather than an individual threat (Pettigrew 2016).

In the 1960s, conceptualization of prejudice gradually changed. While it used to be understood as a psychopathological expression among traditionally minded, conservative, and educationally disadvantaged individuals, it increasingly came to be seen as rooted in socio-psychological processes of social cognition, group dynamics and socialization among ordinary people (Dovidio et al. 2010; Dovidio 2001). With the rise of the civil rights movement and the ensuing promotion of non-discrimination (Civil Rights Act of 1964 in the US and the Race Relation Act of 1965 in the UK), overt expressions of prejudice declined (Schuman et al. 1997). However, it was supplanted by subtle forms of discrimination, consistently observed in North America and in a number of Western European countries (Pettigrew and Meertens 1995). Such subtle discrimination is characterized by ambivalence: majority group members may publicly profess equality while still holding negative attitudes toward minority members in the private sphere, and biases against out-groups might even be implicit or unconscious. They express themselves in non-verbal behavior, less friendly attitudes in interaction with minority groups and aversion toward them (Dovidio et al. 2002).

A range of theories, mainly deriving from the US context, emphasized this transition from overt to more covert or subtle forms of discrimination, such as symbolic racism (Sears and Henry 2003) and modern racism (McConahay 1986). Both of these theories take as their point of departure the conflicting and often ambivalent attitudes of majority group members: humanitarian sympathy for underprivileged persons often goes hand in hand with the blaming of the victims for failing to comply with individualistic values. In this perspective, minority members are resented as they are deemed to ostensibly disregard traditional conservative values (e.g., a

Protestant work ethic) and to make unjustified and excessive claims. Conservatism manifests itself with support for the existing power relations in society and with opposition to policy measures in favor of minority groups.

Aversive racism theory (Gaertner and Dovidio 1986) also deals with subtle, ambivalent attitudes, but focuses on the ambiguities among liberal-minded majority members. While professing equality, those majority individuals still hold conflicting, non-conscious negative feelings about minorities; the resulting discomfort, anxiety, and fears lead to an aversion of contact. Consistent with their non-racist self-image, liberal-minded majority individuals refrain from acting in overtly discriminatory ways; yet, coherent with their unconscious negative attitudes resulting from socialization, they are likely to avoid situations where they come into contact with members of minority groups and tend to refrain from supporting equalizing policies.

Contemporary, subtle forms of discrimination rest on the dissociation between inclusive egalitarian attitudes and unconscious pervasive bias, between controlled responses and automatic responses that can be attributed to immediate associations with an evaluative content. Implicit biases may operate unconsciously to influence behavior. This dissociation model stimulated important methodological developments (Greenwald et al. 1998), suggesting that self-report methods are appropriate for the measure of explicit attitudes but unsuitable for implicit attitudes. Indeed, this research has demonstrated that self-reports and implicit measures of stereotyping and prejudice are largely uncorrelated (Dovidio et al. 2015, 5).

The subtle character of contemporary bias and the impact of implicit attitudes are further at the roots of theories of "color-blind racism" (Bonilla-Silva 2003). To address the effects of implicit bias, well-meaning majority people may emphasize common group identity in a color-blind approach to diversity: they treat individuals as equally as possible, without considering their race, culture, or ethnicity, in order to foster positive intergroup relations. However, common group identity is related to color-blind assimilation ideologies, so that the minority group is expected to conform to dominant norms and values. Color-blind policies tend to preserve white privilege and to maintain minority disadvantages. Stressing color-blindness proves to be a strategical tool: it reinforces hierarchical relations between groups, benefiting high-status majority group members. The other downside of this frame is that it limits awareness of social inequalities, thus it might hamper effective action to address those issues through social change.

3.1.2 Individual-Level Factors in the Labor Market: The Rationale of Gatekeepers

Much research on discrimination aims at understanding the role of differential treatment in the marketplace, such as labor markets, housing markets or the consumer markets (see Chap. 5). While psychologists have approached such market discrimination with the study of stereotypes and attitudes, economists have developed specific theoretical frames to account for discrimination, distinguishing between taste-based and statistical discrimination. In his seminal book, *The Economics of Discrimination* (1957), Becker, for example, discusses the economic effects of racial discrimination in the US labor market. In this book, Becker defines overt racism as individuals' aversion for interracial contact and qualifies it as a "taste" for discrimination. According to Becker, racial discrimination is the result of employers' willingness to pay for not being associated with African Americans – either by rejecting the most productive candidates or by offering a reduced income. In this theoretical model, discrimination is explained with reference to direct racial animus among employers because the behavior lacks "objectivity." Rational behavior is deemed to be based on considerations about productivity alone, and discrimination is thus a result of employers acting based on subjective preferences. As such, an underlying assumption in Becker's theory is that discriminatory employers over time will be crowded out of the labor market because their behavior lowers productivity.

In contrast to the assumption that discrimination and productivity are mutually exclusive, economic models of statistical discrimination, originating from the work of Phelps (1972) and Arrow (1973), rest on the idea that discrimination is a way of managing the imperfect information that characterizes hiring decisions and wage setting in the labor market. According to Phelps, "the employer who seeks to maximize expected profit will discriminate against blacks or women if he believes them to be less qualified, reliable, long-term, etc. on the average than whites and men, respectively, and if the cost of information about the individual applicants is excessive" (Phelps 1972, 659). In the absence of full information, race, ethnicity, and sex will be used as proxies for productivity. According to this theory, risk-aversive employers will hire the candidate who is ascribed membership to the group that has the highest average productivity – presumably whites and men.

The main difference between taste-based and statistical discrimination is the notion of rationality (Midtbøen 2014). Excluding the most productive job applicant on the grounds of race or sex is economically inefficient, while hiring decisions based on estimates of group productivity are assumed to be rational (although still discriminatory) responses to the uncertainty and lack of full information characterizing hiring decisions in the labor market. The employer may reject a suitable candidate because of statistical discrimination, but this cost is traded off against the cost of (trying) to find out the real productivity of all candidates. Both uncertainty and lack of information are inevitable parts of recruitment processes, and a characteristic of organizational behavior as such (Stinchcombe 1990). Nevertheless, an unclear aspect of statistical discrimination models is the question of accuracy in employers' beliefs about average group productivity, which relies heavily on stereotypes. Both Phelps (1972) and Arrow (1973) are somewhat vague on this point, indicating – perhaps – that their models allow for employers' beliefs about blacks and women to be inaccurate depictions of reality and still be "rational" in some sense. Statistical discrimination might thus involve some sort of racist beliefs, even though employers do not consider that they mobilize stereotypes against ethno-racial minorities or women.

To clarify this point, other economists define statistical discrimination as a situation where employers act on the basis of "true stereotypes" (Schwab 1986, 228), arguing strongly that average differences in productivity between whites and blacks, or between men and women, actually exist on average and that this difference is the basis of discrimination (Aigner and Cain 1977). Moreover, an entire branch of the economics literature is concerned with so-called employer learning (e.g., Altonji and Pierret 2001; Farber and Gibbons 1996). These scholars acknowledge that statistical discrimination may be based on outdated beliefs about group productivity, but argue that employers who have positive experiences with stigmatized minority groups will update over time their beliefs to be in accordance with empirical realities (Farmer and Terrell 1996). By effect of a similar learning process, economists would assume that in the long-term employers would better master how to identify the productive candidates, thus reducing statistical discrimination (Midtbøen 2014).

Many sociologists have criticized economic models of statistical discrimination, questioning the idea of accuracy in beliefs about group productivity (e.g., Bielby and Baron 1986; Tomaskovic-Devey and Skaggs 1999), along with the assumption that employers update their views of racial minorities when new and positive information is provided (Pager and Karafin 2009). The idea that employers are guided by "true stereotypes" stands, for example, in striking contrast to the definition of prejudice as "an exaggerated belief associated with a category" (Allport 1954, 191; Fiske 1998). Indeed, important qualitative work both in the US context (e.g., Kirschenman and Neckerman 1991; Moss and Tilly 2001; Shih 2002; Waldinger and Lichter 2003) and in Europe (Friberg 2012; Midtbøen 2014) demonstrates that employers use race and ethnic background as proxies of productivity, but that their views of minority applicants often are based on crude stereotypes. In this regard, England (1992) has made a useful distinction between statistical discrimination, on the one hand, and "error discrimination," on the other, arguing that the latter refers to discriminatory practices guided by erroneous estimates of group averages, typically based on stereotypes about blacks or women. Importantly, however, the notion of error discrimination shares with statistical discrimination the view that employers do not necessarily have a general distaste against particular groups per se, but rather act in a discriminatory way "in an effort to hire a more productive workforce" (England 1992, 60).

3.1.3 Intergroup Relations

While discrimination is often theorized as part of decision-making processes at the individual level, collective phenomena such as stereotypes and prejudices, and their diffusion or change, are also part of the dynamics between individuals and groups. In everyday life, actors inevitably classify people into social categories where new information is assigned to existing categories. This categorization process is useful and even necessary to orient oneself in an environment rich in stimuli, information, and events. However, information confirming one's own conviction tends to be stored, while those contradicting convictions tend to be disregarded, as it disrupts routine and means additional cognitive effort (Nickerson 1998). Categorization assigns individuals to social groups; it often entails the division of social space in an "in-group," which includes the actor of categorization, as opposed to an "out-group." Categorization relies on stereotyping, an inevitable by-product of normal cognitive processes. Stereotypes are "pictures in our heads," according to the famous definitions by Lippmann (1922).

Through categorization, interpersonal behavior becomes intergroup behavior. An individual's self-image results from both personal identity (i.e., what distinguishes one individual from all others) and social identity, the part of the self-concept derived from the consciousness of belonging to one or more groups. According to social identity theory, individuals look for a positive social identity (Tajfel and Turner 1979). As social identity is influenced by group membership, people tend to judge positively the group they belong to and compare it advantageously in relation to out-groups. The preference for the in-group improves the individual's social identity; the identification with the in-group leads to favor it over out-groups, which is often called "in-group favoritism." A group can maintain its higher status by giving privileged treatment to in-group members and reducing access to resources to out-groups. Experimental evidence shows that the simple fact of categorization may arouse intergroup tension between two groups of people randomly assigned to each group who share a common task (Tajfel et al. 1971).

While intergroup contact can lead to stereotyping, prejudice, and discrimination of the out-group, contact theory argues that it may also lead to decreasing prejudice and conflict between majority and minority group members. According to Allport (1954, 281), "[prejudice] may be reduced by equal status contact between majority and minority groups in the pursuit of common goals. The effect is greatly enhanced if this contact is sanctioned by institutional supports (i.e., by law, custom, or local atmosphere), and provided it is of a sort that leads to the perception of common interests and common humanity between members of the two groups). Against Allport's assumption that ethnic antagonism is primarily "a product of fears of the imagination," other authors identify the source of intergroup attitudes and conflict in functional relations between groups and their competition for scarce resources (Katz 1991). When the interests of the groups are interdependent, the group members are supportive and cooperative with each other; when the interests of one's own group and the other groups are in conflict, competition arises. Negative attitudes toward out-groups originate from a feeling of threat (LeVine and Campbell 1972; Esses et al. 2005). Indeed, threat theory is a staple in research on attitudes to immigrants and their descendants.

Realistic conflict theory states that the higher the competition over limited resources, the higher the prejudice and the hostility between groups (Sherif 1966). Integrated threat theory extends the threat derived from the competition on tangible resources like safety, health, economy, and well-being, to the threat perceived on symbolic interests of the in-group, its beliefs, attitudes, and morals, thus echoing social identity theory (Stephan and Renfro 2002). Such threats may target the person or the whole group. A threat is a subjective perception: it does not need to be real. Such perception may, therefore, be constructed by media and public discourse (Brug et al. 2015). The attention to non-economic threats, such as identities, values, and beliefs, has enhanced the threat theory. According to this strand of the literature, the labor market considerations play a less significant role in shaping attitudes toward immigration when values and beliefs are accounted for (Hainmueller and Hopkins 2014).

How attitudes and behavior are linked is a much debated and controversial question. The assumption of a mechanical relationship, supposing that human action is the direct product of conscious mental states, is surely too simple and misleading. In a classical experiment, LaPiere (1934) documented that the articulation of racist attitudes does not need to convert in discriminatory treatment. The weak correspondence between explicit attitudes and behavior is confirmed in numerous studies (e.g., Pager and Quillian 2005; Blommaert et al. 2012). In contrast to the study of LaPiere, however, the disconnection goes more often in the direction of an apparent lack of prejudice and de facto discriminatory decisions. The affective dimension of prejudice (emotional prejudice) is found to be a better predictor of discriminatory behavior than cognitive dimensions (Talaska et al. 2008). The predictive validity of implicit associations as well as their link to discrimination outcomes are also a matter of controversy (Rooth 2010; Oswald et al. 2013; Dovidio et al. 2015; Carlsson and Agerström 2016; Bertrand and Duflo 2016).

In the seminal article "Attitudes vs. Actions", sociologist Richard LaPiere showed that there is "no necessary correlation between speech and action" (1934, 231). The study took the form of an experiment where LaPiere traveled with a Chinese couple through the US in the 1930s, at a time of widespread bigot attitudes against "Orientals." Only in one out of 251 instances did hotel managers refuse the couple accommodation. To provide a comparison between this (at the time) accommodating behavior and reported attitudes, LaPiere questioned 6 months later the same managers whether they would be willing to accommodate distinguished Chinese guests. Their response was overwhelmingly negative; only in one case, the answer was positive.

Brought together, individual theories seek an explanation for the phenomena of discrimination in the personal, internal motivations of perpetrators or in the processes assumed to be similar across countries and therefore universally valid (Guimond et al. 2014). Yet, as we saw, the association of motives and behavior is not straightforward. Underlining the difficulties of measuring motivations, Reskin (2003) recommends shifting the emphasis from individual beliefs and attitudes to the in-depth analysis of social mechanisms; that is, processes that mediate the link between internal states and discriminatory behavior. Many of such social mechanisms are found at the organizational level.

3.2   Organizational-Level Theories

Interpersonal and intergroup encounters always take place in socially structured contexts, making necessary an enlargement of scope to the meso-level of the organizational environment. Organizations – linking the micro and the macro social level – are key structural contexts shaping inequality (Baron and Bielby 1980). Mediating the impact of the individual-level mechanism of discrimination such as cognitive bias and stereotypes of the actors, organizational arrangements govern the extent to which ascriptive characteristics become relevant in determining social outcomes via the distribution of opportunities and rewards. An example in the labor market illustrates this mediating function. Organizational rules influence the degree to which recruiters are informed of ascriptive characteristics, which in turn influence selection-behavior. Facing incomplete information about candidates, recruiters interpret "signals," notably of ascriptive nature, as decision-making tools. Blinding information is, therefore, a tool to curb the impact of unwanted bias. Studying recruitment of musicians in US orchestras, Goldin and Rouse (2000) demonstrated that the adoption of new organizational rules, here "blind auditions," explained 30–50% of the increase of women among new hires. Organizational practices are shaped by societal mechanisms; as such, they might be seen as "the immediate causes of variation in ascriptive inequality" (Reskin 2003, 12).

Tilly (1998) emphasizes the importance of organizational dynamics in creating and maintaining group boundaries. Moreover, he develops an organizational account of "categorical inequalities" (i.e., inequalities across groups of people on the basis of rigid social categories such as gender, race, and immigrant status). According to Tilly, inequalities are not caused by attitudes and beliefs but by the organizational structures and the matching of the exterior (i.e., social) categorical distinctions, to interior organizational distinctions, such as jobs. Interior job distinctions are socially more powerful and generate larger inequalities when they overlap with exterior and culturally legitimate social categories. Distinctions between categories (e.g., men and women, white and black, citizens and non-citizens) are used to both distribute and legitimate inequality. Two complementary mechanisms are primarily responsible for inequalities across social categories: Exploitation, which amounts to unequal distribution of rewards proportionate to value produced, and opportunity hoarding, which amounts to excluding others from access to resources (e.g., jobs). The durability of inequalities depends on their organizational anchoring.

3.2.1   Organizational Procedures: Formalization

Studying the organizational determinants of recruitment has a long history in sociological research. In his famous theory of the modern bureaucracy, Weber (1946), for example, argues that formalized procedures constrain managerial discretion. Merton (1957), too, emphasizes how formal procedures in bureaucracies ensure control over effective decision-making. In the essay "Bureaucratic Structure and Personality," he notes that "specific procedural devices foster objectivity and restrain the 'quick passage of impulse into action'" (Merton 1957, 195).

Organizational and psychosocial theories indicate that the formalization of recruitment and promotion through bureaucratic practices is most likely to counter bias and discretionary decisions in access to employment, as they mediate the impact of individual-level mechanisms (Reskin 2000). Bielby makes this argument most clearly. He argues that "the impact of gender and racial stereotyping on judgments about individuals can be minimized when judgments are based on timely and relevant information; when decision makers evaluate that information consistently with respect to clearly articulated criteria; and when a mechanism exists for holding decision makers accountable for the process they have used and criteria they have applied in making their judgments" (Bielby 2000, 124). Following structural theorists of inequality, mainstream policy recommendations promote formalization of procedures as the proper organizational remedy to harness biased behavior.

However, analyses of observational data measuring the impact of bureaucratic approaches casts doubts on their overall efficacy, suggesting that some approaches being more effective than others (Sturm 2006; Kalev et al. 2006). Controlling managers' discretion and bias proves counterproductive as it may stir resistance and may have adverse effects. In their studies aimed at assessing the effectiveness of antidiscrimination organizational policies, Dobbin and Kalev (2013) and Dobbin et al. (2015) identify the creation of formal organizational responsibility in charge of developing equal opportunity programs ensuring internal compliance to the regulatory frame as crucial tools to enhance the diversity of the workforce. Transparency of the allocation process and open accountability for the decisions proved also effective in increasing diversity.

3.2.2 Organizational Mechanisms: Networks as Opportunity Hoarding

Because of their mediating role, organizational structures may attenuate categorical distinctions – as with formalized procedures – or indeed accentuate them. This is the case when employees' referrals are used largely in the recruitment process. While cost-effective and promising a better fit of newcomers in the workforce, this practice of activating internal networks, however, might prove to be a mechanism for ensuring in-group preference and promoting "homosocial reproduction" (Kanter 1977), whereby the dominant group favors and gives advantages to individuals carrying their ascriptive characteristics, in terms of ethnic background, racial appearance, and sex.

Resorting to networks to fill a position amounts to monopolization of resources by the established group to the detriment of "outsider" groups. Such referral practices result in the exclusion of categorically distinct others from jobs: as a mechanism of "opportunity hoarding" (Tilly 1998), it powerfully contributes to the reproduction of existing inequalities. Boulton (2015) provides an empirical example of this mechanism with his qualitative analysis of three large advertising agencies and their practices in the allocation of highly sought-after internships, which constitute a crucial point of entry into the labor market. Under the cover of color-blind meritocracy, influent players place friends and relatives, thus ensuring the material advantage of the established racial group.

As aptly noticed (Voss 2010), this mechanism is close to Weber's idea of social closure. Networks are effective ways in not only gaining access to employment (as well as housing or services), but also in securing further education, informal mentoring, and other tools leading to career advancement. Although apparently neutral, activation of networks results in powerful instruments of cumulative (dis-)advantage.

3.2.3   Organizational Environment: The Regulatory Framework

Organizational practices are shaped by societal mechanisms. The mediating function of organizations derives also from the fact that they represent the implementing level of general policy orientations. Describing the history of corporate policies and tools in the US, Dobbin and Kalev (2013) illustrate how the macro regulatory frame was responsible for the implementation of antidiscrimination policies at the corporate level and influenced the way those policies evolved over time. In the UK, the institution of the Commission for Racial Equality in 1976, on the basis of the Race Relation Act, has progressively made the regulatory framework for businesses and public services more precise and stringent. In the EU, the 2000 Directive "implementing the principle of equal treatment between persons irrespective of racial or ethnic origin" (2000/43/CE) and the one "establishing a general framework for equal treatment in employment and occupation" (2000/78/CE) have similarly shaped the regulatory frame inspiring national legislation influencing organizational setups (see Chap. 7).

While the analysis of the regulatory frame has stimulated a vast literature, the impact of its enforcement is less developed. A crucial issue in this respect is how extensively and effectively the regulatory frame succeeds in preventing discrimination. Assuming that employers discriminate, consciously or unconsciously, as long as this is de facto possible, Petersen and Saporta (2004) shift their analysis to the conditions under which discriminatory practices in hiring, salary, promotion, or departures are more expected to occur. Analyzing the whole career development of employees in a large US service organization, they find that the hiring process appears as presenting the widest "opportunity structure for discrimination." It is the most exposed to risks of discrimination because this is where the chance of employers being "caught in the act" is most limited (see also Bendick Jr. and Nunes 2012, 242–243).

While Petersen and Saporta analyze the room left uncovered by the regulatory frame, Hirsch (2009) focuses on the mechanisms ensuring efficacy to such a frame. Studying the direct impact and indirect pressure of legal and judicial enforcement of antidiscrimination legislation in the US, she shows that the case-by-case regulatory approach is not directly effective on the sanctioned discriminatory companies. Yet, sanctions exert an indirect pressure by creating a normative environment promoting gender and racial equality: "the driving force of the law is not sanctions but the legal environment they create" (Hirsch 2009, 245). However, gender desegregation has proven more sensitive to this normative pressure than race desegregation, as enforcement efforts in the latter respect lack sustained political support in comparison with those for sex desegregation (Hirsch 2009, 268). In the EU, the implementation of the directives at the corporate level is quite limited. With these insights in mind, it is not surprising that in their meta-analysis Zschirnt and Ruedin (2016) reported no difference in levels of hiring discrimination before and after the introduction of the EU directives.

Becoming aware of the mediating role of organizations has a bearing on the research agenda on discrimination: insights from social psychological research on prejudice and stereotypes are thus coupled with sociological research on the dynamics of organizations and institutions, providing analyses in which the organizational contexts of discrimination are moved to the forefront of this field of research. Yet, in turn, organizations are situated in larger social, economic, political, and legal environments exerting a powerful influence on the organizational settings.

3.3 Structural-Level Theories

Structural discrimination shifts the attention precisely toward such broader societal structures. The contextual dimension neglected in early theories (Fiske 1998) provides tools to understand variations in discrimination across time and space and the way it is produced and reproduced by institutions. Compared to individual and organizational theories, a structural discrimination approach expands the analysis of discrimination usually confined to one domain and a point in time in the two significant directions of time and scope (Pager and Shepherd 2008). Time, by emphasizing the production and reproduction of inequality into enduring self-perpetuating phenomenon through racial bias. Scope, by transcending unequal treatment in a specific domain, and paying attention to the interrelations among various domains affecting the entire society.

3.3.1 Present as Sediment of the Past

The advantages of one individual or group over another accumulates over time, reinforcing disparities so that the inequality of this advantage grows over time. Merton (1968) speaks in this regard of the "Matthew effect," referring to the "parable of the talents" in the Book of Matthew. Cumulative advantage presents an affinity to theories of social stratification and reproduction linking social class origin to allocation mechanisms and social outcomes, reproducing the society class structure (Bourdieu and Passeron 1990). The cumulative advantage is the unequal growth rate in an outcome for individuals holding different statuses and growing inequality over time in a status group.

The cumulative disadvantage is the reverse side of the cumulative advantage (DiPrete and Eirich 2006). In its most frequent sense in sociology, the process of cumulative disadvantage is understood as the combination of direct and indirect effects of group membership on outcomes (negative for minority groups in relation to the majority) at different stages in the life course (Blank 2005). Cumulative disadvantage focuses on differential outcomes over time within a particular context, emphasizing dynamic processes that reinforce disparate outcomes. Blau and Duncan (1967) developed this concept in their classical study of *The American Occupational Structure*, yet it may easily be applied to similar cumulative disparities among ethnic groups.

When the timespan considered exceeds the lifespan to encompass generational succession, the attention shifts to history. Historical practices and policies of intentional discrimination project their gloomy shade into the present time through the mechanism of cumulative disparities. Therefore, historical experiences of exclusion may actualize disadvantage over time. This sort of structural discrimination is known as "past-in-present discrimination" (Williams 2000). Affirmative action policies were designed to counter the phenomenon's inertia of this disadvantage (Wrench 2007).

In the US, the history of slavery and institutionalized racial segregation affects structures of disadvantage particularly concerning the African American population (Massey and Denton 1993; Pager and Shepherd 2008; Alexander and Rucker Jr. 2010). In many European countries, such as Britain, France, and the Netherlands, large migration inflows in the post-war era came from former colonies echoing the longstanding history of imperialism and colonialism (Castles et al. 2014).

Europe's colonial past also has a bearing on contemporary patterns of racism: histories of exploitation directly affect ethnic relations through representations, ideologies, and practices that convey negative perceptions of minorities as inferiors and deny them full membership in the majority community (Bancel et al. 2010; Gilroy 1987, 2005; Oostindie 2008; Back and Solomos 2000; Thomas 2013; Amiraux and Simon 2006). Racism and anti-immigrant sentiment in Europe are also related to the economic and social consequences of the economic crisis in the 1970s and, later, to the focus on security and global terrorism following September 11, 2001. The combination of large-scale migration and a revival of nationalism and its symbols have created a situation that systematically works in disfavor of migrants in general, and of the Muslim population in Western countries, in particular (Castles et al. 2014).

3.3.2 Cumulative Interrelated Processes

Analyses of discrimination at the societal level expand further in a second direction by enlarging the scope of the analysis to cumulative processes. If cumulative disadvantage focuses on differential outcomes over time within a particular context, Blank goes beyond the dynamic progression with her concept of cumulative discrimination, defined as "discriminatory effects over time and across domains" (Blank 2005, 2; Blank et al. 2004).

Discrimination may indeed cumulate across processes within a domain of social life, such as the labor market: discrimination in hiring or work assignments, for instance, may affect promotion prospects and wage growth. Moreover, discrimination in one social domain may have spillover effects from one domain another. Consider as an example, the following sequence of effects: Discrimination in housing shapes residential patterns (Massey and Denton 1993). Such patterns, in turn, affect the concentration of minority students in schools, in traditional catchment area systems, where students are assigned to a public school depending on the geographical area in which they are domiciled. The combined impact of the socioeconomic and the ethnic composition of the school have an effect on student performance (Karsten 2010) and, in turn, unemployment risks (Heath and Cheung 2007; Heath et al. 2008). Furthermore, residential patterns have an impact of occupation: unemployment rates are higher when job opportunities are located far away from the neighborhoods where people live (spatial mismatch; Duguet et al. 2009; Kain 1968). Blank et al. (2004) thus enlarge the scope of the analysis to encompass the interrelations among different domains, stressing the systematic aspect of the cumulative process. However, acknowledging the difficulty of the task, scholars regret that research in this direction is rare.

Blank et al. (2004) theorize cumulative discrimination as disadvantages across time and domains combined with causal analysis. Reskin (2012) similarly embeds it in a "system perspective" with her notion of "*über* discrimination" (see Chap. 2). According to Reskin, sociologists have been too concerned with patterns of discrimination in particular social areas, preventing high-quality analyses from addressing the "reciprocal causality of disparities across spheres" (Reskin 2012, 18). The lack of a systems perspective on racial inequality in mainstream quantitative research renders invisible the potential feedback effects by which patterns of disadvantage are transferred across time and domains, and, as a result, prevents policy interventions from advancing racial justice. Reskin thus calls for increased attention to the relations among subsystems, of the feedback effects reinforcing disparities across subsystems, sustained by beliefs and values influencing the distribution of resources.

3.3.3 Institutional Discrimination as a Result of State Policies and Practices

If cumulative processes in time and scope build the core of structural discrimination, Pager and Shepherd (2008) subsume under this label also a somewhat different conceptualization, often labeled "institutional discrimination." They define it as "the range of policies and practices that contribute to the systematic disadvantage of members of certain groups" (Pager and Shepherd 2008, 197), be they carried out by state or non-state institutions toward racialized or ethnicized groups.

Embedded in the radical black tradition that can be traced back to W. E. B. Du Bois, the theory of institutional racism was originally formulated by Carmichael and Hamilton (1967). In their analysis of the disadvantage of blacks in the US, they show no interest in intentions and interpersonal situations but focus on the effects of socially established power relations. Carmichael and Hamilton claim that racist practices are at the heart of ordinary practices; racism, therefore, finds its place in its daily banality, without the need for justification. In this perspective, racism is inherent in the very functioning of society, embedded in routine mechanisms ensuring the domination of certain groups. Because of its routinization, there is no need for any scientific theory or justification. Institutional racism is "less overt, far more subtle, and less identifiable in terms of specific individuals committing the acts. However, it is no less destructive of human life. It originates in the operation of established and respected forces in the society and thus receive less public condemnation" (Carmichael and Hamilton 1967, 20). In this perspective, racism is part of the very functioning of society, ensuring through routine mechanisms the domination of already privileged groups.

As pointed out in the previous chapter, the concept of "systemic racism" is very close to institutional racism. It refers "to the foundational, large-scale and inescapable hierarchical system of US racial oppression devised and maintained by whites and directed at people of color" (Feagin and Elias 2013, 936). Systemic racism is a "material, social, and ideological reality that is well embedded in major US institutions" (Feagin 2006, 2). However, grounded in the race-critical literature, it adds to it the notion of the white frame, "a socially constructed, meta-structure shaping and pervading not only the 'state' but also the 'economy' and 'civil society'" (Feagin and Elias 2013, 937) permeating all aspects of US society. The white frame concept confers materiality and visibility to the actual majority, white promoters of systemic racism, otherwise hidden behind abstract references to "society." Systemic racism here differs from the organizational systemic discrimination discussed at the organizational level, as it emphasizes societal-power unbalances and the role of perpetrators and perpetuators of racist practices as causes of inequalities.

This contextual, institutionally embedded dimension of discrimination has found high resonance in various European countries, with an increasing focus on discrimination in systems of equality (see Chap. 5). The concept of "institutionalized racism" made its way to the UK as applied to colonial immigration. It is prominently featured in the Macpherson Report of 1999, resulting from the judicial enquiry in the murder of a young black person in an unprovoked, racist attack and in the failure of the police investigations into this murder. The report presented to Parliament by the Secretary of State for the Home Department heavily criticizes those investigations as "marred by a combination of professional incompetence, institutional racism and a failure of leadership by senior officers" (Home Office 1999, para 6.34). The authors outline this concept as follows: "The collective failure of an organization to provide an appropriate and professional service to people because of their color, culture, or ethnic origin. It can be seen or detected in processes, attitudes, and behavior which amount to discrimination through unwitting prejudice, ignorance, thoughtlessness and racist stereotyping which disadvantage minority ethnic people" (Home Office 1999, para 6.34).

In Germany, the concept is adopted under the label of institutional discrimination (Gomolla 2017) to designate the production of inequalities by institutions intended to provide services equal services to all individuals (see Chap. 5). Gomolla and Radkte (2000) theorize institutional discrimination in their analyzing of school failure of children of immigrants. The core of the matter lies not in prejudice or the intention to discriminate of the parties involved, but in the durable and systematic nature of relative disadvantages produced by the school structure and functioning. Analyzing statistically measurable effects of the unequal distribution of educational success by ethnic differences, Gomolla and Radkte (2009) shift the attention away from the individual and the interactional levels toward the legal and political framework conditions, the organizational and financial aspects, the structures, programs, norms, rules, and routines as well as collective knowledge repertoires supporting decision-making. They focus on institutions in the Durkheimian sense, as a system of social relations with certain stability over time, with collective ways of acting and thinking and with their own existence outside individuals. From the perspective of institutional discrimination, critical questioning of existing institutions works as a programmatic tool and lays the foundations for the search for reforms and affirmative action policies aiming at justice and equity (Gomolla 2017).

As for France, "the existence of systemic racism within certain institutions (particularly the police, schools, social housing, and public health services) produces widespread discriminations and contributes to segregation" (Amiraux and Simon 2006, 206). Yet the development of the genuine sociology of ethnic minorities has been hindered by the French, republican integration model. This is both a political fact and a largely dominant "a-racial" (Amiraux and Simon 2006, 204) analytical referent, based on the principle of in-differentiation and assimilation. The heated debate about the use of ethnic and racial categories in statistics is symptomatic in this respect (Simon 2015).

Remarkably, scientific attention and political sensitivity to ascriptive inequality of immigrant-origin groups in Europe grow parallel to their long-term settlement in European immigration societies, revealed by the emergence of migrant offspring as a social reality and political actor. Yet in today's immigration countries, group hierarchies are institutionally anchored in state policies and practices. Regulation of immigration increasingly diversifies status tracks, thus producing a "legal stratification of immigration status." "Immigration and citizenship laws continue to create hierarchies among migrants that mirror the intersection of non-meritocratic attributes of social group membership such as gender, race/ethnicity nationality, religion and class" (Ellermann and Goenaga 2019, 2).

In the highly stratified political and economic international system of nation-states, the automatic acquisition of citizenship by birth determines critically unequal access to resources for individuals. In a provocative book, *The Birthright Lottery*, Shachar (2009) develops the analogy between birthright citizenship in rich societies and the inheritance of property, which opens access to rights and secures privileges. By virtue of this comparison, birthright citizenship amounts to an ascriptive attribute in the face of global inequalities. As such, it contributes to the production and reproduction of inequality into a self-perpetuating phenomenon nurturing processes of cumulative advantage. Making this point, Shachar shows us yet another example of structural discrimination.

3.4   Conclusion

This overview of main theories in the field shows the complexity of discrimination phenomena, reflecting such pervasive domination relationships that they materialize at every level of analysis of social behavior – individual, organizational, and structural. In spite of these different levels of analysis, the various theories of discrimination reviewed share a common feature, namely the fact that discrimination maintains privileges of certain ascribed groups over others. As such, discrimination helps to reproduce existing power relations among groups and consequently perpetuates ethnic and racial hierarchies. Perpetrators – consciously or not – make use of their power to engage in discrimination to uphold their privileges at the detriment of individuals and groups in a less favorable position in the social hierarchy.

For a long time in Europe, the dominant frame to understand social and economic inequality was social stratification without references to ethno-racial diversity. This interpretative frame was applied also to labor immigration after World War II. Yet the changing features of immigration (settlement of early migrant populations, development of migrant and refugee flows at a larger global scale, descendants of immigrants coming of age) combined with deep socioeconomic transformations of receiving societies have gradually uncovered how social hierarchies are intertwined with and overlap with ethnic and racial hierarchies. Indeed, Fassin and Fassin's (2006), *From the social question to the racial question?*, is the evocative title of a stimulating essay pointing in this direction.

The multi-layered theoretical approaches show the importance of the macrosocial dimension. The European context is diverse by the number of countries yet similar to its normative frame lends itself for comparative studies aiming at highlighting the relevance of the structural and institutional dimensions shaping forms and scope of ascriptive inequality.

References

Adorno, T. W., Frenkel-Brunswik, E., Levinson, D. J., Nevitt Sanford, R., Aron, B. R., Levinson, M. H., & Morrow, W. R. (1950). *The authoritarian personality*. New York: Harper.
Aigner, D. J., & Cain, G. G. (1977). Statistical theories of discrimination in labor markets. *Industrial and Labor Relations Review, 30*(2), 175–187.

Alexander, L. M., & Rucker, W. C., Jr. (Eds.). (2010). *Encyclopedia of African American history*. Santa Barbara: ABC-CLIO.

Allport, G. (1954). *The nature of prejudice*. Cambridge, MA: Addison-Wesley.

Altonji, J. G., & Pierret, C. R. (2001). Employer learning and statistical discrimination. *The Quarterly Journal of Economics, 116*(1), 313–350.

Amiraux, V., & Simon, P. (2006). There are no minorities here: Cultures of scholarship and public debate on immigrants and integration in France. *International Journal of Comparative Sociology, 47*(3–4), 191–215.

Arrow, K. (1973). The theory of discrimination. In O. Ashonfelter & A. Rees (Eds.), *Discrimination in labor markets* (pp. 15–42). Princeton: Princeton University Press.

Back, L., & Solomos, J. (2000). *Theories of race and racism: A reader*. London: Routledge.

Bancel, N., Bernault, F., Blanchard, P., Boubeker, A., Mbembe, A., & Vergès, F. (2010). *Ruptures postcoloniales: les nouveaux visages de la société Française*. Paris: La Découverte.

Baron, J. N., & Bielby, W. T. (1980). Bringing the firms Back in: Stratification, segmentation, and the organization of work. *American Sociological Review, 45*, 737–765.

Becker, G. S. (1957). *The economics of discrimination*. Chicago: Chicago University Press.

Bendick, M., Jr., & Nunes, A. P. (2012). Developing the research basis for controlling bias in hiring. *Journal of Social Issues, 68*(2), 238–262. https://doi.org/10.1111/j.1540-4560.2012.01747.x.

Bertrand, M., & Duflo, E. (2016). *Field experiments on discrimination*. Cambridge, MA: National Bureau of Economic Research. NBER Working Paper No. 22014.

Bielby, W. T. (2000). Minimizing workplace gender and racial bias. *Contemporary Sociology: A Journal of Reviews, 29*, 120–129. https://doi.org/10.2307/2654937.

Bielby, W. T., & Baron, J. N. (1986). Men and women at work: Sex segregation and statistical discrimination. *American Journal of Sociology, 91*(4), 759–799. https://doi.org/10.1086/228350.

Blank, R. M. (2005). Tracing the economic impact of cumulative discrimination. *American Economic Review, 95*(2), 99–103.

Blank, R. M., Dabady, M., & Citro, C. F. (Eds.). (2004). *Measuring racial discrimination. Panel on methods for assessing discrimination*. Washington, DC: National Research Council, National Academies Press.

Blau, P. M., & Duncan, O. D. (1967). *The American occupational structure*. New York: Wiley.

Blommaert, L., van Tubergen, F., & Coenders, M. (2012). Implicit and explicit interethnic attitudes and ethnic discrimination in hiring. *Social Science Research, 41*(1), 61–73.

Bonilla-Silva, E. (2003). Racial attitudes or Racial ideology? An alternative paradigm for examining actors' Racial views. *Journal of Political Ideologies, 8*(1), 63–82. https://doi.org/10.1080/13569310306082.

Boulton, C. (2015). Under the cloak of whiteness: A circuit of culture analysis of opportunity hoarding and colour–blind racism inside US advertising internship programs. *tripleC: Communication, Capitalism & Critique, 13*(2), 390–403.

Bourdieu, P., & Passeron, J.-C. (1990). *Reproduction in education, society, and culture* (2nd ed.). London: Sage.

Brug, W. v. d., D'Amato, G., Berkhout, J., & Ruedin, D. (Eds.). (2015). *The politicisation of migration*. London: Routledge.

Carlsson, R., & Agerström, J. (2016). A closer look at the discrimination outcomes in the IAT literature. *Scandinavian Journal of Psychology, 57*(4), 278–287. https://doi.org/10.1111/sjop.12288.

Carmichael, S., & Hamilton, C. V. (1967). *Black power: The politics of liberation in America*. New York: Vintage.

Castles, S., de Haas, H., & Miller, M. J. (2014). *The age of migration: International population movements in the modern world* (5th ed.). Basingstoke: Palgrave Macmillan.

DiPrete, T. A., & Eirich, G. M. (2006). Cumulative advantage as a mechanism for inequality: A review of theoretical and empirical developments. *Annual Review of Sociology, 32*, 271–297.

Dobbin, F., & Kalev, A. (2013). The origins and effects of corporate diversity programs. In Q. M. Roberson (Ed.), *The Oxford handbook of diversity and work* (pp. 253–281). Oxford: Oxford University Press.

Dobbin, F., Schrage, D., & Kalev, A. (2015). Rage against the iron cage: The varied effects of bureaucratic personnel reforms on diversity. *American Sociological Review, 80*(5), 1014–1044. https://doi.org/10.1177/0003122415596416.

Dovidio, J. F. (2001). On the nature of contemporary prejudice: The third wave. *Journal of Social Issues, 57*(4), 829–849. https://doi.org/10.1111/0022-4537.00244.

Dovidio, J. F., Kawakami, K., & Gaertner, S. L. (2002). Implicit and explicit prejudice and interracial interaction. *Journal of Personality and Social Psychology, 82*(1), 62. https://doi.org/10.1037/0022-3514.82.1.62.

Dovidio, J. F., Hewstone, M., Glick, P., & Esses, V. M. (2010). Prejudice, stereotyping, and discrimination. In J. F. Dovidio, M. Hewstone, P. Glick, & V. M. Esses (Eds.), *The SAGE handbook of prejudice, stereotyping, and discrimination* (pp. 3–29). Los Angeles: Sage.

Dovidio, J. F., Gaertner, S. L., & Saguy, T. (2015). Color-blindness and commonality: Included but invisible? *American Behavioral Scientist, 59*(11), 1518–1538. https://doi.org/10.1177/0002764215580591.

Duguet, E., L'Horty, Y., & Sari, F. (2009). Sortir du chômage en Île-de-France. *Revue économique, 60*(4), 979–1010.

Ellermann, A., & Goenaga, A. (2019). Discrimination and policies of immigrant selection in Liberal states. *Politics and Society, 47*(1), 87–116. https://doi.org/10.1177/0032329218820870.

England, P. (1992). *Comparable worth: Theories and evidence.* Piscataway: Transaction Publishers.

Esses, V. M., Dovidio, J. F., Danso, H. A., Jackson, L. M., & Semenya, A. (2005). Historical and modern perspectives on group competition. In C. S. Crandall & M. Schaller (Eds.), *Social psychology of prejudice: Historical and contemporary issues* (pp. 97–115). Lawrence: Lewinian Press.

Farber, H. S., & Gibbons, R. (1996). Learning and wage dynamics. *The Quarterly Journal of Economics, 111*(4), 1007–1047. https://doi.org/10.2307/2946706.

Farmer, A., & Terrell, D. (1996). Discrimination, Bayesian updating of employer beliefs, and human capital accumulation. *Economic Inquiry, 34*(2), 204–219.

Fassin, D., & Fassin, E. (2006). *De la question sociale à la question raciale? Représenter la société Française.* Paris: La Découverte.

Feagin, J. R. (2006). *Systemic racism: A theory of oppression.* New York: Routledge.

Feagin, J., & Elias, S. (2013). Rethinking racial formation theory: A systemic racism critique. *Ethnic and Racial Studies, 36*(6), 931–960. https://doi.org/10.1080/01419870.2012.669839.

Fiske, S. (1998). Stereotyping, prejudice, and discrimination. In D. Gilbert, S. Fiske, & G. Lindzey (Eds.), *The handbook of social psychology* (pp. 357–411). New York: McGraw Hill.

Friberg, J. H. (2012). Culture at work: Polish migrants in the ethnic division of labour on Norwegian construction sites. *Ethnic and Racial Studies, 35*(11), 1914–1933.

Funke, F., Petzel, T., Cohrs, C., & Duckitt, J. (Eds.). (2016). *Perspectives on authoritarianism.* Cham: Springer.

Gaertner, S. L., & Dovidio, J. F. (1986). *The aversive form of racism.* San Diego: Academic.

Gilroy, P. (1987). *There Ain't no black in the union Jack: The cultural politics of race and nation.* London: Hutchinson.

Gilroy, P. (2005). *Postcolonial melancholia.* New York: Columbia University Press.

Goldin, C., & Rouse, C. (2000). Orchestrating impartiality: The impact of "blind" auditions on female musicians. *American Economic Review, 90*(4), 715–741. https://doi.org/10.1257/aer.90.4.715.

Gomolla, M. (2017). Direkte und indirekte, institutionelle und strukturelle Diskriminierung. In A. Scherr, A. El-Mafaalani, & G. Yüksel (Eds.), *Handbuch Diskriminierung* (pp. 134–155). Wiesbaden: Springer.

Gomolla, M., & Radtke, F.-O. (2000). Mechanismen institutionalisierter Diskriminierung in der Schule. In I. Gogolin & B. Nauck (Eds.), *Migration, gesellschaftliche Differenzierung und Bildung* (pp. 321–341). Opladen: Leske + Budrich.

Gomolla, M., & Radtke, F.-O. (2009). *Institutionelle Diskriminierung: die Herstellung ethnischer Differenz in der Schule*. Wiesbaden: Springer.

Greenwald, A. G., McGhee, D. E., & Schwartz, J. L. K. (1998). Measuring individual differences in implicit cognition: The implicit association test. *Journal of Personality and Social Psychology, 74*(6), 1464. https://doi.org/10.1037/0022-3514.74.6.1464.

Guimond, S., de la Sablonnière, R., & Nugier, A. (2014). Living in a multicultural world: Intergroup ideologies and the societal context of intergroup relations. *European Review of Social Psychology, 25*(1), 142–188. https://doi.org/10.1080/10463283.2014.957578.

Hainmueller, J., & Hopkins, D. J. (2014). Public attitudes toward immigration. *Annual Review of Political Science, 17*, 225–249. https://doi.org/10.1146/annurev-polisci-102512-194818.

Heath, A. F., & Cheung, S. Y. (Eds.). (2007). *Unequal chances: Ethnic minorities in Western labour markets*. Oxford: British Academy/Oxford University Press.

Heath, A. F., Rothon, C., & Kilpi, E. (2008). The second generation in Western Europe: Education, unemployment, and occupational attainment. *Annual Review of Sociology, 34*, 211–235. https://doi.org/10.1146/annurev.soc.34.040507.134728.

Hirsch, C. E. (2009). The strength of weak enforcement: The impact of discrimination charges, legal environments, and organizational conditions on workplace segregation. *American Sociological Review, 74*(2), 245–271. https://doi.org/10.1177/000312240907400205.

Home Office. (1999). *The Stephen Lawrence inquiry: Report of an inquiry by Sir William Macpherson of Cluny*. London: Stationery Office.

Kain, J. (1968). Housing segregation, negro employment, and metropolitan decentralization. *Quarterly Journal of Economics, 82*, 175–197. https://doi.org/10.2307/1885893.

Kalev, A., Dobbin, F., & Kelly, E. (2006). Best practices or best guesses? Assessing the efficacy of corporate affirmative action and diversity policies. *American Sociological Review, 71*(4), 589–617. https://doi.org/10.1177/000312240607100404.

Kanter, R. M. (1977). *Men and women of the corporation*. New York: Basic Books.

Karsten, S. (2010). School segregation. In the Organisation for Economic Co-operation and Development (OECD) (Ed.), *Equal opportunities? The labour market integration of children of immigrants* (pp. 195–210). Paris: OECD.

Katz, I. (1991). Gordon Allport's 'The nature of prejudice'. *Political Psychology, 12*(1), 125–157.

Kirschenman, J., & Neckerman, K. M. (1991). We'd love to hire them, but...: The meaning of race for employers. In C. Jencks & P. E. Peterson (Eds.), *The urban underclass* (pp. 203–232). Washington, DC: Brookings Institution.

LaPiere, R. T. (1934). Attitudes vs. Actions. *Social Forces, 13*(2), 230–237. https://doi.org/10.2307/2570339.

LeVine, R. A., & Campbell, D. T. (1972). *Ethnocentrism: Theories of conflict, ethnic attitudes, and group behavior*. Oxford: Wiley.

Lippmann, W. (1922). *Public opinion*. New York: MacMillan Co.

Massey, D. S., & Denton, N. (1993). *American apartheid: Segregation and the making of the underclass*. Cambridge, MA: Harvard University Press.

McConahay, J. B. (1986). Modern racism, ambivalence, and the modern racism scale. In J. F. Dovidio & S. L. Gaertner (Eds.), *Prejudice, discrimination, and racism* (pp. 91–125). Boulder: Academic.

Merton, R. K. (1957). Bureaucratic structure and personality. In *Social theory and social structure* (pp. 195–206). Glencoe: Free Press.

Merton, R. K. (1968). The Matthew effect in science. *Science, 159*(3810), 56–63.

Midtbøen, A. H. (2014). The invisible second generation? Statistical discrimination and immigrant stereotypes in employment processes in Norway. *Journal of Ethnic and Migration Studies, 40*(10), 1657–1675. https://doi.org/10.1080/1369183X.2013.847784.

Moss, P., & Tilly, C. (2001). *Stories employers tell: Race, skill, and hiring in America*. New York: Russell Sage Foundation.

Nickerson, R. S. (1998). Confirmation bias: A ubiquitous phenomenon in many guises. *Review of General Psychology, 2*(2), 175–220. https://doi.org/10.1037/1089-2680.2.2.175.

Oostindie, G. (Ed.). (2008). *Dutch colonialism, migration and cultural heritage: Past and present*. Leiden: KITLV Press.

Oswald, F. L., Mitchell, G., Blanton, H., Jaccard, J., & Tetlock, P. E. (2013). Predicting ethnic and racial discrimination: A meta-analysis of IAT criterion studies. *Journal of Personality and Social Psychology, 105*(2), 171. https://doi.org/10.1037/a0032734.

Pager, D., & Karafin, D. (2009). Bayesian bigot? Statistical discrimination, stereotypes, and employer decision making. *The Annals of the American Academy of Political and Social Science, 621*(1), 70–93. https://doi.org/10.1177/0002716208324628.

Pager, D., & Quillian, L. (2005). Walking the talk? What employers say versus what they do. *American Sociological Review, 70*(3), 355–380. https://doi.org/10.1177/000312240507000301.

Pager, D., & Shepherd, H. (2008). The sociology of discrimination: Racial discrimination in employment, housing, credit, and consumer markets. *Annual Review of Sociology, 34*, 181–209. https://doi.org/10.1146/annurev.soc.33.040406.131740.

Petersen, T., & Saporta, I. (2004). The opportunity structure for discrimination. *American Journal of Sociology, 109*(4), 852–901. https://doi.org/10.1086/378536.

Pettigrew, T. F. (2016). In pursuit of three theories: Authoritarianism, relative deprivation, and intergroup contact. *Annual Review of Psychology, 67*(1), 1–21. https://doi.org/10.1146/annurev-psych-122414-033327.

Pettigrew, T. F., & Meertens, R. W. (1995). Subtle and Blatant Prejudice in Western Europe. *European Journal of Social Psychology, 25*(1), 57–75. https://doi.org/10.1002/ejsp.2420250106.

Phelps, E. S. (1972). The statistical theory of racism and sexism. *The American Economic Review, 62*(4), 659–661.

Reskin, B. F. (2000). Getting it right: Sex and race inequality in work organizations. *Annual Review of Sociology, 26*(1), 707–709. https://doi.org/10.1146/annurev.soc.26.1.707.

Reskin, B. F. (2003). Including mechanisms in our models of ascriptive inequality. *American Sociological Review, 68*, 1–21. https://doi.org/10.1007/1-4020-3455-5_4.

Reskin, B. F. (2012). The race discrimination system. *Annual Review of Sociology, 38*, 17–35. https://doi.org/10.1146/annurev-soc-071811-145508.

Rooth, D.-O. (2010). Automatic associations and discrimination in hiring: Real world evidence. *Labour Economics, 17*(3), 523–534. https://doi.org/10.1016/j.labeco.2009.04.005.

Roscigno, V. J., Garcia, L. M., & Bobbitt-Zeher, D. (2007). Social closure and processes of race/sex employment discrimination. *The ANNALS of the American Academy of Political and Social Science, 609*(1), 16–48. https://doi.org/10.1177/0002716206294898.

Schuman, H., Steeh, C., Bobo, L., & Krysan, M. (1997). *Racial attitudes in America: Trends and interpretations*. Cambridge, MA: Harvard University Press.

Schwab, S. (1986). Is statistical discrimination efficient? *The American Economic Review, 76*(1), 228–234.

Sears, D. O., & Henry, P. J. (2003). The origins of symbolic racism. *Journal of Personality and Social Psychology, 85*(2), 259. https://doi.org/10.1037/0022-3514.85.2.259-.

Shachar, A. (2009). *The Birthright lottery: Citizenship and global inequality*. Cambridge, MA: Harvard University Press.

Sherif, M. (1966). *Group conflict and cooperation: Their social psychology*. London: Routledge and Kegan Paul.

Shih, J. (2002). Yeah, I could hire this one, but I know it's Gonna be a problem': How race, nativity, and gender affect employers' perceptions of the manageability of job seekers. *Ethnic and Racial Studies, 25*(1), 99–119. https://doi.org/10.1080/01419870120112076.

Simon, P. (2015). The choice of ignorance: The debate on ethnic and racial statistics in France. In P. Simon, V. Piché, & A. A. Gagnon (Eds.), *Social statistics and ethnic diversity* (pp. 65–87). Cham: Springer.

Stephan, W. G., & Renfro, C. L. (2002). The role of threat in intergroup relations. In D. M. Mackie & E. R. Smith (Eds.), *From prejudice to intergroup emotions: Differentiated reactions to social groups* (pp. 191–207). New York: Psychology Press.

Stinchcombe, A. L. (1990). *Information and organizations*. Berkeley: University of California Press.

Sturm, S. (2006). The architecture of inclusion: Advancing workplace equity in higher education. *Harvard Journal of Law & Gender, 29*(2), 247. Available at SSRN: https://ssrn.com/abstract=901992.

Tajfel, H., & Turner, J. C. (1979). An integrative theory of intergroup conflict. In W. G. Austin & S. Worchel (Eds.), *The social psychology of intergroup relations* (pp. 33–47). Belmont: Nelson-Hall.

Tajfel, H., Billig, M. G., Bundy, R. P., & Flament, C. (1971). Social categorization and intergroup behaviour. *European Journal of Social Psychology, 1*(2), 149–178. https://doi.org/10.1002/ejsp.2420010202.

Talaska, C. A., Fiske, S. T., & Chaiken, S. (2008). Legitimating Racial discrimination: Emotions, not beliefs, best predict discrimination in a meta-analysis. *Social Justice Research, 21*(3), 263–296. https://doi.org/10.1007/s11211-008-0071-2.

Thomas, D. (2013). *Africa and France: Postcolonial cultures, migration, and racism*. Bloomington: Indiana University Press.

Tilly, C. (1998). *Durable inequality*. Berkeley: University of California Press.

Tomaskovic-Devey, D., & Skaggs, S. (1999). An establishment-level test of the statistical discrimination hypothesis. *Work and Occupations, 26*(4), 422–445. https://doi.org/10.1177/0730888499026004003.

Voss, K. (2010). Enduring legacy? Charles Tilly and durable inequality. *The American Sociologist, 41*(4), 368–374. https://doi.org/10.1007/s12108-010-9113-yK.

Waldinger, R., & Lichter, M. I. (2003). *How the other half works: Immigration and the social Organization of Labor*. Berkeley: University of California Press.

Weber, Max. 1946. "Bureaucracy." In From Max Weber: Essays in sociology, Hans Heinrich Gerth and Charles Wright Mills, 196–264. New York: Oxford University Press.

Williams, Melissa S. 2000. "In defence of affirmative action: North American discourses for the European context?" In Combating Racial Discrimination: Affirmative action as a model For Europe, Erna Appelt and Monica Jarosch, 61–79. Oxford: Berg.

Wrench, J. (2007). *Diversity management and discrimination: Immigrants and ethnic minorities in the EU*. Aldershot: Ashgate.

Zschirnt, E., & Ruedin, D. (2016). Ethnic discrimination in hiring decisions: A meta-analysis of correspondence tests 1990 –2015. *Journal of Ethnic & Migration Studies, 42*(7), 1115–1134. https://doi.org/10.1080/1369183X.2015.1133279.

Chapter 4
Methods of Measurement

Documenting the extent to which discrimination exists, why it occurs, and how it effects individual life chances is a crucial but difficult task. It is crucial because the magnitude of discrimination, at least to a certain extent, defines its salience as a political issue. It is difficult because no method of measurement is without flaws. Indeed, decades of research in sociology, economics, and social psychology have dealt with questions of discrimination, using a wide range of methodological approaches, and providing strong evidence that discrimination occurs. However, no single method is able to grasp the full picture. Different methods provide insights into different aspects of the discrimination complex, suggesting that they are complementary approaches rather than competing.

This chapter reviews the strengths and weaknesses of the most commonly used methods of measurement in the field of discrimination research. Taking as its point of departure how we can assess the extent to which discrimination occurs, the chapter reviews quantitative and qualitative analyses of experiences, attitudes, legal complaints, and residual gaps, as well as different forms of experimental designs. A key point in the chapter is to show that although all of these methods shed light on discrimination, they are useful for answering somewhat different questions. Consequently, careful consideration of the range of methods available is necessary for matching one's research question with the appropriate research design.

4.1 Experiences of Discrimination

The perhaps most intuitive approach to studying discrimination is to ask members of underprivileged groups whether they have experienced differential treatment based on their personal characteristics, which in the context of this book means their ethnic, racial, or religious background. Such studies are conducted in many national contexts, typically by including questions about discrimination in survey questionnaires, such as in the French Trajectories and Origins survey (Beauchemin et al.

© The Author(s) 2021   43
R. Fibbi et al., *Migration and Discrimination*, IMISCOE Research Series,
https://doi.org/10.1007/978-3-030-67281-2_4

2018) or the Norwegian Living conditions among immigrants' survey (Statistics Norway 2017). Questions about experiences of discrimination are also included in several comparative surveys, at the EU level most notably in the European Union Minorities and Discrimination Surveys (EU-MIDIS), conducted in 2008 and 2016. Additionally, discrimination is covered in the European Social Survey (ESS), but in the ESS, respondents are asked whether they believe that they belong to a group that is discriminated against in the country of residence, rather than if they have experienced discrimination themselves. Of course, asking respondents about individual experiences or their experience of being a member of a discriminated group do not measure the same phenomenon. For example, it is possible to consider oneself a member of a discriminated minority group, such as Muslims in Europe, while never having had any personal experiences of differential treatment. Indeed, there is a tendency in the literature that the levels of perceived group discrimination are higher than the level of personal experiences (e.g., Skrobanek 2009).

Several Eurobarometer surveys also include questions about discrimination. Here, respondents are asked whether they think that discrimination against specific groups are widespread in their own country, whether they have personal experiences of discrimination, and whether they have witnessed discrimination as a third party. Since these questions clearly measure different aspects of discrimination, it should come as no surprise that the results vary strongly depending on the question posed. For example, the Eurobarometer report *Discrimination in the EU in 2015* (European Commission 2015) shows that while, at the aggregate level, 64% of the respondents believe that discrimination against ethnic minorities is widespread in their own country, only 3% of the respondents had personally experienced discrimination. Among the ethnic minorities in the sample, however, 30% had personal experiences of discrimination.

Besides large-scale surveys, experiences of discrimination may also be studied by conducting ethnographic work or in-depth interviews among potential target groups. The advantage of such qualitative approaches, compared to surveys, is that the researcher gets the opportunity to dig more deeply into the forms, locations, and consequences of discrimination. Many qualitative studies show that discrimination can take quite subtle forms, which may be difficult to capture by standardized survey questionnaires. Additionally, qualitative research can provide important glimpses into how experiences of discrimination shape future action, for example by investigating what strategies individuals develop to avoid discrimination (e.g., Kang et al. 2016; Lamont et al. 2016; see also Chap. 6). Though qualitative studies cannot produce results that are generalizable to a broader population, they are invaluable in providing the researcher with rich data that increases our understanding of the discrimination complex.

The great advantage of studying experiences of discrimination is that such data documents important aspects of the living conditions of individuals and groups in society. Large-scale surveys can shed light on the prevalence of experiences of discrimination and whether such experiences vary by conditions such as place of residence, level of education, and type of work. Survey data also allows for comparing variations of discrimination between different minority groups and how discrimination on the basis of ethnicity, race, or religion intersects with discrimination based on gender, age, health status, or sexual orientations – what we referred to as intersectional discrimination in Chap. 2. When using longitudinal survey designs, it is also possible to investigate the long-term effects of discrimination on, for example, the level of well-being, mental health, feelings of belonging to majority society, job search strategies, as well as key integration outcomes such as employment and income. Qualitative studies, on the other hand, can provide a deeper understanding of the forms of discrimination involved, what reactions such experiences create, and what kind of strategies individuals develop to avoid future discrimination.

Yet, a major problem of experience-based studies, especially concerning surveys, is the inavailability of high-quality data. Potential target groups are often small and typically underrepresented in population-wide surveys, leading to biased measures of discrimination. Even with high-quality data, however, there remain uncertainties concerning the measure of discrimination provided. Whether individuals perceive an action or situation as discriminatory is largely subjective. Moreover, perceptions may depend on individuals' consciousness of their exposure to unfair treatment. Individuals might interpret the same situation differently, according to their expectations, their sensitivity and frames of reference, and of course their previous experiences. Furthermore, in selection processes such as job recruitment, the decision-making is not observed directly by the applicant, making it hard to detect whether a rejection is due to discrimination or based on legitimate criteria. Hence, studies of experiences of discrimination can result in both over- and under-estimation of the actual extent of discrimination.

4.2 Attitudinal Studies

Another important line of discrimination research deals with the opposite source of the phenomenon, by considering attitudes toward immigrants and ethnic minorities. Questions about the views of minority groups, perceptions of how the integration or diversity policies work and whether all groups should be offered equal opportunities in society, are part of many population-wide surveys. Such surveys provide useful insights into general attitudes in society, how attitudes differ from country to country, and – through repeated measurement – whether attitudinal changes occur over time.

Studies of attitudes toward immigration are regularly conducted at both the national level and the EU level. One out of many examples is a report based on rounds 1 and 7 of the ESS (Heath and Richards 2016), which compares attitudes among representative samples of the populations in 21 European countries. The report finds that attitudes toward immigration have gradually become more positive over time. Yet there are large differences between countries; the Scandinavian populations display the most positive attitudes while inhabitants in the Czech Republic and Hungary are the most negative. The report also shows a clear hierarchy of minority groups: Jewish people are more welcome than Muslims, who again are more welcome than Roma. Furthermore, highly educated migrants are preferred to low-educated migrants, and low-educated migrants from European countries are preferred to those from outside Europe. Although such numbers do not shed direct light on discrimination patterns, both cross-country differences and the existence of group hierarchies provide useful insights into prevailing sentiments that may shape access to opportunities for minority groups. A recent Swedish study of housing discrimination (Carlsson and Eriksson 2017), for example, shows that landlords are more likely to discriminate in regions where people are more negative toward ethnic minorities, suggesting that reported attitudes expressed in surveys indeed might be a useful predictor of instances of ethnic discrimination.

Of course, it is also possible to measure discrimination more directly, for instance in employment, by conducting surveys or in-depth interviews with employers and asking concrete questions about their hiring practices. A range of studies conducted in both the US and Europe show that employers can be surprisingly outspoken when it comes both to their perceptions about minority groups and in accounting for their considerations in recruitment processes. In a seminal study among Los Angeles employers' attitudes toward African American and Latino low-educated workers, for example, Johanna Shih (2002) found that a central concern of employers is control at the workplace. The employers in Shih's study consequently sought workers whom they perceived as manageable and pliable. As perceptions of this kind are not only based on individual merit or employers' assessments of single applicants, but also vary along categorical lines such as race and gender, studies such as this show how stereotypes at the group level might affect the employment prospects of minority workers.

To be sure, a range of similar studies has been conducted in the European context, not least in the field of low-skilled employment and studies of immigrant niches in the lower tiers of European labor markets. Employers in such labor markets tend to have limited information about individual applicants and therefore often use categorical characteristics such as gender, age, ethnicity, nationality, immigration status or race as a proxy for skills (Friberg and Midtbøen 2018; Moss and Tilly 2001). Importantly, though these processes might be especially salient in low-wage labor markets, they are not limited to them, and stereotypical assessments of specific immigrant groups might affect both the employment prospects of other groups as well as of later generations. Indeed, as Midtbøen (2014) found in a qualitative study among Norwegian employers, stereotypes associated with immigrants seem to be inferred from ethnically distinct names, and negative experiences are regularly generalized between ethnic groups and across generations. The implications of such dynamics for children of immigrants are potentially severe: Instead of experiencing equal access to the labor market, they encounter attitudes and stereotypes attached to their parents' generation, making their domestic educational qualifications and linguistic fluency "invisible" in the eyes of employers.

Clearly, studies that directly examine gatekeepers' attitudes are a valuable source of knowledge about discriminatory practices. However, it is not easy to establish a clear relationship between attitudes and actions. As mentioned in Chap. 3, LaPiere (1934) found, in a classic experiment, that hotel receptionists in the US in practice were more indifferent to racial minorities than they said they would be when prompted with direct questions. However, recent studies have shown that the opposite might be equally true. In a seminal study, Pager and Quillian (2005) explored the relationship between American employers' actions and attitudes by matching data from an experimental audit study with a telephone survey among the same employers. The authors found that although the employers in the survey claimed that they would not discriminate against African American job applicants, the experiment showed large racial disparities in chances of landing a job. This suggests that interviews among potential perpetrators of discrimination leaves open the question of the reliability of the accounts gathered by the researcher.

Furthermore, important discussions in the current field of discrimination research, as discussed in Chap. 3, is whether discrimination occurs deliberately or unconsciously and whether discriminatory practices can be mediated by rules and procedures at the organizational level, such as standardized applications and transparent decision-making processes. Although one can capture a bit of the conscious motivations behind gatekeepers' actions through surveys and in-depth interviews, such accounts are not necessarily reliable indicators of the actual level of discrimination.

4.3 Studies of Legal Complaints

A different source of knowledge about discrimination is formal complaints put forward to courts or public bodies such as the Equal Employment Opportunity Commission (EEOC) in the US, the Employment Tribunal in Britain, or the Antidiscrimination Tribunal in Norway. In many countries, official records documenting claims of discrimination and the legal treatment of the complaints are accessible to researchers through an application. These records provide an interesting glimpse into the types of discrimination that are claimed, how the volume and content of claims change over time, and how antidiscrimination policies are enforced in specific contexts.

Studies of legal claims are most frequently conducted in the US context, and this body of work clearly demonstrates that such claims represent an interesting entry to studies of discrimination. For example, in the book *The Face of Discrimination: How Race and Gender Impact Work and Home Lives* (2007), Vincent J. Roscigno uses narrative data from employment and housing claims submitted to the Ohio Civil Rights Commission. Roscigno finds that the highest number of claims come from the low-wage service sector and that firing discrimination is the most important claim in the private sector, whereas, in the public sector, discrimination in hiring, promotion, and firing are evenly distributed. Looking specifically into race and gender differences, Roscigno also shows that while white women are more likely to report discrimination due to pregnancy, black women tend to report more frequently instances of racial discrimination than discrimination related to their experiences as women. Altogether, the book builds on more than 14,000 verified discrimination cases as well as qualitative analyses of about 850 of the same cases, including in-depth studies of how employers and plaintiffs narrate their positions in cases with disputed outcomes.

As this book demonstrates, legal cases may provide insight into both the concrete management of the discrimination legislation and the different parties'reasoning. Legal cases typically also offer detailed descriptions of a range of different situations, and they include the legal assessment made in each case. When a large amount of cases is available, it is also possible to look in depth into the intersections of race, class, and family statuses, as well as comparing similarities and differences between the public and the private sector.

Despite their merits, studies of legal complaints have some major drawbacks. Most importantly, few incidents of discrimination actually end up in the legal system. This is especially the case in national settings with an underdeveloped (or even non-existent) public grievance system. Furthermore, putting forward a legal claim requires time and resources, and that victims of discrimination believe that they would find reparation with legal action. Discrimination cases frequently fail to be successful in the legal system, because firm evidence is hard to provide. In this context of uncertainty, victims might not see the benefits of putting a claim in justice. Finally, discriminatory actions and decisions are often hidden from the ones affected by it, suggesting that most discriminatory acts go under the legal radar. Consequently, though studies of this kind represent an important source of knowledge about the nature of discrimination, legal reports are less useful as indicators of the overall extent of discrimination occurring in a specific national context.

4.4 Studies of Residual Gaps

As discrimination is part of, but not the sole driver of, creating and maintaining ethnic inequalities, a key question in much social science research is the actual role that discrimination plays in shaping access to opportunities. How much, say, of the unemployment rates that exist between the native and the foreign-born population in a country can be explained by human capital factors such as differences in the level of education and language proficiency, and how much is due to discrimination in hiring processes?

To answer such questions, discrimination is often measured indirectly as the unequal access to positions or resources – such as jobs, wages, housing, selective education tracks – by statistical analyses of large data sets. In these types of studies, the focus is not on the experiences that individuals or groups have with discrimination or on the attitudes of the dominant group. Rather, the researcher takes as the point of departure the mean distribution of groups on a specific dependent variable, such as wages, unemployment, or occupational attainment, and then controls for relevant, non-discriminatory factors that could explain the observed group differences, such as school performance, level of education, and work experience. The residual gap remaining between groups in a given outcome is usually referred to as "ethnic penalties"; that is, the disadvantages facing ethnic minorities compared to majority peers after controlling for (most) productivity-relevant factors.

A vast body of work builds on this "residual method." One influential example is *Unequal Chances: Ethnic Minorities in Western Labour Markets* (2007), a comparative volume edited by Anthony Heath and Sin-Yi Cheung. This book compares patterns of unemployment and occupational attainment for a range of different ethnic groups of both the first and second generation in altogether 13 countries, including Austria, Britain, Canada, France, Germany, the Netherlands, Sweden, and the US. The book demonstrates that in all countries examined, non-European minority groups face ethnic penalties in accessing the labor market and that these disadvantages are transferred across generations despite the educational progress achieved by children of immigrants. Further, the book shows that there is a considerable cross-national variation in the magnitude and scope of ethnic penalties. In some contexts, such as in Britain and Sweden, disadvantages appear to be reserved to the labor market entrance, while in others, such as in Germany and Austria, ethnic penalties are also present later in the employment relationship, suggesting a pattern of cumulative disadvantage in labor market trajectories in some context but not in others.

Statistical analyses of group differentials, such as in *Unequal Chances*, are of utmost importance in providing large-scale pictures of ethnic inequalities, as well as in differentiating between relevant factors explaining gaps in a given outcome. However, it is important to have in mind that ethnic penalties are not equivalent to ethnic discrimination. Indeed, because the role of discrimination in studies using the residual method is not examined directly, but rather is left as part of the unexplained residual, there is always uncertainty regarding the existence of unobserved factors that might explain the remaining difference between the groups, such as ethnic differentials in access to relevant social networks. Some studies attempt to isolate the effect of social networks and thus come closer to a "clean" measure of discrimination, but the direct role of discrimination in explaining ethnic differentials in labor market outcomes remains nevertheless unresolved in studies of this type.

4.5   Experimental Studies

The limitations of traditional methods in assessing the direct role of discrimination in access to opportunities in employment and housing have paved the way for the increasing use of experimental approaches. Indeed, the strength of experimental approaches to studies of discrimination is the ability to isolate causal effects; that is, the direct effect of a racial appearance or a minority-ethnic sounding name on, for example, the chances of landing a job. In a randomized, controlled experiment, subjects are randomly assigned to clearly defined "treatment" and "control" conditions in order to control for every other factor potentially influencing the outcome of interest. As such, experimental studies, when conducted carefully, are able to examine the role of discrimination directly.

Experimental approaches to discrimination come in different forms. One much-debated method is the so-called "Implicit Association test" (IAT), in which participants in quick succession are presented pictures of different categories of people (women and men, elderly and young, white and black) and asked to connect these pictures to positively and negatively charged properties (see Chap. 3). The idea is to investigate whether individuals more quickly associate stereotypical (often negative) characteristics to traditional "out-groups" than to "in-groups" (e.g., Greenwald et al. 1998).

Another approach is survey experiments or so-called vignettes. A typical example is studies where respondents are asked to assess whether they would hire a particular person or what they would offer to the person in pay. In such studies, the formal qualifications of the fictitious person in question are held constant, but respondents are randomly given persons with different names or different racial appearance, to measure the effect of that isolated variable on the respondents' decision (e.g., Pedulla 2014). Another version of this method is to include an experimental element as part of ordinary survey questionnaires, for example, to investigate whether respondents vary in tolerance when confronted with different groups. Toril Aalberg et al. (2012), for example, conducted a survey experiment to examine whether the willingness to admit individuals as legal immigrants depends on their attributes. Using an experimental design in the Norwegian context, specific attributes of immigrants were manipulated, making them appear more or less likely to make an economic contribution and more or less likely to assimilate into Norwegian culture. The authors found that the decision to admit individuals were influenced by the immigrant's economic background, in which Norwegians were especially supportive of highly skilled immigrants, but also that immigrants with an Afrocentric appearance were more likely to be rejected by men, but accepted by women.

The most direct measure of discrimination, however, is provided by field experiments. Field experiments of discrimination can be divided into two main categories or techniques: Audit studies and correspondence test studies. In audit studies, pairs of individuals who differ in racial markers but are carefully matched in relevant productivity characteristics and trained to act similarly, apply for real-world jobs or housing vacancies by showing up in person (e.g., Pager 2003). In correspondence test studies, matched pairs of résumés and cover letters differing in the names of the applicants (signaling different race or ethnicity) are sent in response to job openings or to housing offers (e.g., Bertrand and Mullainathan 2004). In both types of studies, the effect of race or ethnicity on opportunities is directly measured. Because all factors other than race or ethnicity are isolated and the résumés are randomly assigned to the test persons, well-conducted field experiments provide convincing estimates of the incidence of discrimination in specific markets.

More than 100 field experiments of ethnic and racial discrimination in employment have been conducted all over the world, but predominantly in North America and Western Europe. Results have varied across countries, but not one single study has concluded that discrimination is *not* a relevant factor in shaping access to employment for a variety of racial and ethnic minority groups. In several countries, minority applicants have to apply to twice as many applications to get job interview offers compared to equally qualified majority peers. However, there is an interesting variation across national contexts (e.g. Di Stasio et al. 2019). A recent meta-analysis of field experiments by Eva Zschirnt and Didier Ruedin (2016), for example, shows that discrimination levels are lower in German-speaking countries than in other countries, probably reflecting the high amount of information required to apply for jobs in these contexts. Another meta-analysis, conducted by Lincoln Quillian et al. (2019), compares the countries where most field experiments have been conducted, demonstrating that the level of racial discrimination in the US is significantly lower than the discrimination against ethnic minorities in France.

Recently, the meta-analysis technique has also been used to investigate trends in discrimination over time in single countries. In the US, where most field experiments have been conducted, Quillian et al. (2017) find that there has been no change in the level of discrimination against African Americans over the past 25 years, suggesting a distressing persistence of discrimination patterns. The same pattern is documented in Britain, where a recent meta-analysis of all field experiments conducted between 1967 and 2017 found no reduction in the level of discrimination against black Caribbean and Asian minorities over a fifty-year time span (Heath and Di Stasio 2019).

Importantly, these overall negative effects of racial and ethnic minority background on employment opportunities conceal important variations in the results of single field experiments and countries. One such dimension is whether different minority groups constitute an "ethnic hierarchy" in which some groups (e.g., white immigrant-origin groups) are systematically preferred over "visible" or racialized minorities of non-European origin. Many studies do indeed point to the existence of such hierarchies and, in those cases, applicants with backgrounds from North Africa and the Middle East tend to be most severely disadvantaged. In a few other studies, by contrast, no ethnic hierarchy is identified (e.g., McGinnity and Lunn 2011). Still, when taking all studies together, the level of discrimination against white immigrants and their descendants are significantly lower than the discrimination against racially visible minority groups (Quillian et al. 2019).

The obvious advantage of experimental approaches over non-experimental studies is the researcher's extensive control over the variables in play. By isolating an "ethnic variable," as in field experiments, or manipulating the link between names and specific characteristics, as in survey experiments, it is possible to draw causal inferences about the effect of ethnic background on, say, wage setting or callbacks for a job interview. The disadvantage of laboratory and survey experiments is external validity: Because the research is conducted in artificial settings, it is difficult to assess whether the results obtained may be generalized to the real world. Field experiments, by contrast, allow researchers to retain the ability to draw causal inferences while staging the research in real-world settings like hiring processes ensures that conclusions are relevant to actual social contexts. Nevertheless, even field experiments face limitations. Although these studies have convincingly documented the fact that discrimination occurs, this research tradition has been less productive in explaining the *processes* by which race and ethnicity become factors of importance in employers' decision-making (Pager et al. 2009; Midtbøen 2015). This means that a field experiment can demonstrate the causal effect of a foreign name on employment prospects, but unless it is complemented with other methods it cannot shed much light on the mechanisms leading to discriminatory practices.

4.6 Conclusion

This chapter has briefly reviewed the most commonly used methods and approaches in research on discrimination. The key take-away message is that the suitability of methods depend on the question posed: A focus on people's experiences highlights central aspects of everyday life, studies of potential discriminators can provide insights into the way individuals in power positions make their decisions, and studies of residual gaps are of indisputable importance in providing large-scale pictures of ethnic inequalities in key outcomes such as unemployment, occupational attainment, education, housing, or health. To assess the direct role of discrimination in shaping groups' access to opportunities in the labor or housing market, however, field experiments are considered the "gold standard." As each approach to the study of discrimination nevertheless suffers from certain limitations, the more widespread use of research designs that combine different methods in single studies would be much welcome.

References

Aalberg, T., Iyengar, S., & Messing, S. (2012). Who is a 'deserving' immigrant? An experimental study of Norwegian attitudes. *Scandinavian Political Studies, 35*(2), 97–116. https://doi.org/10.1111/j.1467-9477.2011.00280.x.

Beauchemin, C., Hamel, C., & Simon, P. (Eds.). (2018). *Trajectories and origins: Survey on the diversity of the French population* (INED population studies, Vol. 8). Cham: Springer.

Bertrand, M., & Mullainathan, S. (2004). Are Emily and Greg more employable than Lakisha and Jamal? A field experiment on labor market discrimination. *The American Economic Review, 90*(4), 991–1013. https://doi.org/10.1257/0002828042002561.

Carlsson, M., & Eriksson, S. (2017). Do attitudes expressed in surveys predict ethnic discrimination? *Ethnic and Racial Studies, 40*(10), 1739–1757. https://doi.org/10.1080/01419870.2016.1201580.

Di Stasio, V., Lancee, B., Veit, S., & Yemane, R. (2019). Muslim by default or religious discrimination? Results from a cross-National Field Experiment on hiring discrimination. *Journal of Ethnic and Migration Studies*. https://doi.org/10.1080/1369183X.2019.1622826.

European Commission. (2015). *Discrimination in the EU in 2015* (Special Eurobarometer, Vol. 437). Brussels: European Commission.

Friberg, J. H., & Midtbøen, A. H. (2018). Ethnicity as skill: Immigrant employment hierarchies in Norwegian low-wage labour markets. *Journal of Ethnic and Migration Studies, 44*(9), 1463–1478. https://doi.org/10.1080/1369183X.2017.1388160.

Greenwald, A. G., McGhee, D. E., & Schwartz, J. L. K. (1998). Measuring individual differences in implicit cognition: The implicit association test. *Journal of Personality and Social Psychology, 74*(6), 1464. https://doi.org/10.1037/0022-3514.74.6.1464.

Heath, A., & Di Stasio, V. (2019). Racial discrimination in Britain, 1969–2017: A meta-analysis of field experiments on racial discrimination in the British labour market. *British Journal of Sociology*. https://doi.org/10.1111/1468-4446.12676.

Heath, A., & Richards, L. (2016). *Attitudes toward immigration and their antecedents: Topline results from round 7 of the European Social Survey*. ESS Topline Results Series. Retrieved from: https://www.europeansocialsurvey.org/docs/findings/ESS7_toplines_issue_7_immigration.pdf%20

Kang, S. K., DeCelles, K. A., Tilcsik, A., & Jun, S. (2016). Whitened resumes: Race and self-presentation in the labor market. *Administrative Science Quarterly, 61*(3), 469–502. https://doi.org/10.1177/0001839216639577.

Lamont, M., Silva, G. M., Welburn, J., Guetzkow, J., Mizrachi, N., Herzog, H., & Reis, E. (2016). *Getting respect: Responding to stigma and discrimination in the United States, Brazil, and Israel*. Princeton: Princeton University Press.

LaPiere, R. T. (1934). Attitudes vs. actions. *Social Forces, 13*(2), 230–237. https://doi.org/10.2307/2570339.

McGinnity, F., & Lunn, P. D. (2011). Measuring discrimination facing ethnic minority job applicants: An Irish experiment. *Work, Employment & Society, 25*(4), 693–708. https://doi.org/10.1177/0950017011419722.

Midtbøen, A. H. (2014). The invisible second generation? Statistical discrimination and immigrant stereotypes in employment processes in Norway. *Journal of Ethnic and Migration Studies, 40*(10), 1657–1675. https://doi.org/10.1080/1369183X.2013.847784.

Midtbøen, A. H. (2015). The context of employment discrimination: Interpreting the findings of a field experiment. *The British Journal of Sociology, 66*(1), 193–214. https://doi.org/10.1111/1468-4446.12098.

Moss, P., & Tilly, C. (2001). *Stories employers tell: Race, skill, and hiring in America*. New York: Russell Sage Foundation.

Pager, D. (2003). The mark of a criminal record. *American Journal of Sociology, 108*(5), 937–975. https://doi.org/10.1086/374403.

Pager, D., & Quillian, L. (2005). Walking the talk? What employers say versus what they do. *American Sociological Review, 70*(3), 355–380. https://doi.org/10.1177/000312240507000301.

Pager, D., Western, B., & Bonikowski, B. (2009). Discrimination in a low-wage labor market: A field experiment. *American Sociological Review, 74*, 777–799. https://doi.org/10.1177/000312240907400505.

Pedulla, D. (2014). The positive consequences of negative stereotypes: Race, sexual orientation, and the job application process. *Social Psychology Quarterly, 77*(1), 75–94. https://doi.org/10.1177/0190272513506229.

Quillian, L., Hexel, O., Pager, D., & Midtbøen, A. H. (2017). Meta-analysis of field experiments shows no change in racial discrimination in hiring over time. *Proceedings of the National Academy of the Sciences in the United States, 114*(41), 10870–10875. https://doi.org/10.1073/pnas.1706255114.

Quillian, L., Heath, A., Pager, D., Midtbøen, A. H., Fleischmann, F., & Hexel, O. (2019). Do some countries discriminate more than others? Evidence from 97 field experiments of racial discrimination in hiring. *Sociological Science, 6*, 467–496. https://doi.org/10.15195/v6.a18.

Shih, J. (2002). '… Yeah, I could hire this one, but I know it's Gonna be a problem': How race, nativity, and gender affect employers' perceptions of the manageability of job seekers. *Ethnic and Racial Studies, 25*(1), 99–119. https://doi.org/10.1080/01419870120112076.

Skrobanek, J. (2009). Perceived discrimination, ethnic identity and the (Re-) ethnicisation of youth with a Turkish ethnic background in Germany. *Journal of Ethnic and Migration Studies, 35*(4), 535–554. https://doi.org/10.1080/13691830902765020.

Statistics Norway. (2017). *Levekår blant innvandrere i Norge 2016* (SSB-report 2017/13). Oslo/ Kongsvinger: Statistics Norway.

Zschirnt, E., & Ruedin, D. (2016). Ethnic discrimination in hiring decisions: A meta-analysis of correspondence tests 1990 –2015. *Journal of Ethnic & Migration Studies, 42*(7), 1115–1134. https://doi.org/10.1080/1369183X.2015.1133279.

Chapter 5
Discrimination Across Social Domains

Discrimination can take place in all spaces and places where people interact. However, a careful look into the large body of empirical work that can be grouped under the heading "discrimination research" suggests that the concepts, theories, and methods employed vary significantly across studies. This variation is not simply a matter of the individual researchers' likes and dislikes regarding concepts, theories, or methods. Both the forms of discrimination and how it can be measured vary across social domains, depending on whether the domain in question is based primarily on what we here coin "systems of differentiation" or "systems of equality". Social domains that involve some kind of market transaction – such as employment or housing – are heavily dominated by processes of selection and differentiation. By contrast, social domains such as schools, health systems or public services should, in essence, provide all individuals with equal assistance. The different logics inherent in systems of differentiation and systems of equality have implications for the forms of discrimination located and the conclusions reached in studies.

This chapter builds on the distinction between systems of differentiation and systems of equality, reviewing a selection of studies of discrimination in various social domains. It does not aim at providing an exhaustive review of existing research, but to group studies according to the type of social domain in which discrimination occurs. This way of categorizing research demonstrates that there is an interesting interplay between social domains and their respective rationale (differentiation/equality), the types of methods employed and the forms of discrimination detected. The chapter concludes by a critical reflection on the ability of social science research to capture forms of discrimination that are less easy to spot.

© The Author(s) 2021
R. Fibbi et al., *Migration and Discrimination*, IMISCOE Research Series,
https://doi.org/10.1007/978-3-030-67281-2_5

5.1   Systems of Differentiation vs. Systems of Equality

Most market transactions involve some kind of differential treatment. When applying for a job or trying to rent an apartment, individuals normally compete with others in a more or less open market. To get access to the goods in question they need to appear qualified and attractive to employers or landlords – who can choose from a pool of candidates based on a set of formal and informal criteria. Sometimes, these criteria are quite formal and explicit – such as in many advertisements for vacant jobs – while in other cases, the criteria are informal and implicit, such as in the private housing market. Although both employers and property owners in most countries are bound by law not to discriminate against individuals based on characteristics such as race or ethnicity, market transactions of this kind nonetheless include selection, and thus an element of differential treatment, since not all applicants can rent a home or be offered a job. One or a few will always be granted access to particular goods at the expense of others who want the same. Whether or not this unavoidable differentiation is discriminatory depends on whether the choice of candidate is based on legitimate or illegitimate criteria; that is, whether the decision is based on formal qualifications or, say, influenced by the racial appearance or ethnic background of the candidates.

The element of differential treatment that is inherent in most market transactions does not exist in a similar manner in all social domains. The school system, for example, shall provide an education of good quality to all regardless of ethnic background or other characteristics. Likewise, public bodies such as health services or welfare offices shall offer equal services to increasingly diverse populations. Of course, direct discrimination may occur in these social domains as well. For example, teachers may favor students who share their ethnic background or religious beliefs and let this in-group favoritism come to the disadvantage of students of other ethnicities or religions. Similarly, welfare workers or public advisors might provide members of minority groups with less information about their rights to social benefits, for instance, because of a more or less conscious perception that certain groups are "less deserving" of public goods than others are. Yet the modus operandi in systems of equality is not selection. Individuals or groups do not compete over access to scarce goods similar to labor or housing markets. In fact, in systems of equality, market transactions (at least ideally) do not play a role at all. The absence of differential treatment as a key form of human action in systems of equality might suggest that direct discrimination is less prevalent. At a minimum, discrimination in such systems is less clear-cut than in systems of differentiation, and it is far more difficult to detect because the interaction takes place in spaces where researchers' direct access to relevant processes of the interaction is limited.

This somewhat schematic distinction between systems of differentiation and systems of equality is useful when assessing the methods and theories used and the forms of discrimination most frequently reported in different strands of research. However, what goes missing in the distinction is social domains characterized by law enforcement, such as the police, customs, and the judiciary system – what could perhaps be coined "systems of control". These are all social domains that rest on principles of equality for the law, yet extant research suggests that differentiation based on ethnic and racial appearance – what is often called "racial" or "ethnic profiling" – indeed takes place, for example in identity checks (e.g., FRA 2010; Jobard et al. 2012). In the remainder of this chapter, however, we will stick to the simple distinction between systems of differentiation and systems of equality, as the main intent is to show how the logic or functions of these two systems shape our knowledge about the prevalence and forms of discrimination.

The European Union Agency for Fundamental Rights (FRA) defines 'discriminatory ethnic profiling' as 'the practice of basing law enforcement decisions solely or mainly on an individual's race, ethnicity or religion' (FRA 2010, 6). According to Robert Staples (2011), in the US context, the phenomenon in which racialized minorities are exposed to racial profiling dates back to the age of slavery and the awareness and critique of such practices have been present for decades. In Europe, the awareness of ethnic profiling is more recent, and often connected to policing and especially to counter-terrorism enforcement in the aftermath of 9/11, 2001, and later terror attacks in cities such as Madrid (2004), London (2005, 2017), and Paris (2015, 2016). Empirical studies have substantiated the biases in policing and sanctioning against ethno-racial minorities, such as in France, where an experimental survey in two main transportation hubs in Paris found that blacks were between 3.3 and 11.5 times more likely than whites to be stopped, and Arabs between 1.8 and 14.8 more times (Goris et al. 2009). This study shows that young men with a minority background who wear "urban style" cloths are targeted at particularly high rates.

5.2 Discrimination Research in Systems of Differentiation

In domains where gatekeepers regulate the access to certain goods based on competition between individuals– such as jobs in labor markets and rental contracts in housing markets – discrimination can be directly assessed by experimental approaches, and particularly by field experiments. The virtue of field experiments was explained in Chap. 4: By manipulating information about fictitious applicants' race or ethnicity, while holding all other information constant, such studies allow the researcher to measure the direct effect of the chosen characteristic on the relative chance of being invited to a job interview, getting an offer of renting an apartment or getting a mortgage loan offer, compared to equally qualified native-majority applicants. Indeed, field experiments have proven very efficient in documenting the prevalence of discrimination in various social domains, yet almost exclusively in social domains characterized by systems of differentiation, such as labor, housing, and product markets, where the researcher can intervene in naturally occurring selection processes.

In a field experiment of housing discrimination in Italy, for example, Baldini and Federici (2011) investigated whether individuals of different gender and ethnic backgrounds are discriminated against when trying to access the rental market. The authors created twelve fictitious individuals – four with Italian-sounding names, four with Arab/Muslim names and four with East European-sounding names – and sent emails from these individuals to vacant rental apartments in altogether 41 Italian cities. In total, more than 3600 emails were sent in response to vacant apartments. The results show that, on average, Italian-named individuals received a positive reply from landlords in 62% of the cases, while the Arab- and Eastern European-named individuals received positive responses in 44% and 50% of the cases, respectively. These differences are all statistically significant. The results further show that discrimination is higher against male foreign names, in particular for the Arab-named group. Further, discrimination against foreign names appears to be higher in Northern Italy than in other parts of the country, again particularly against Arab males (for reviews of all field experiments of housing discrimination, see Auspurg et al. 2019; Riach and Rich 2002; Rich 2014).

Similar findings are recorded in field experiments in the labor market, where the researcher typically creates fictitious job applicants with ethnically distinguishable names. Bursell (2014), for example, sent more than 3600 job applications to vacant labor market positions in Sweden. The fictitious male and female job applicants had Swedish, Arabic, and North African names, but had identical qualifications. Bursell found that the foreign-named applicants had significantly lower chances of receiving callbacks for job interviews: The overall relative callback rate was 1.8, meaning that while the Swedish-named applicants had to apply for ten jobs before being contacted by an employer, the foreign-named applicants had to apply eighteen times to receive a callback. The study shows no differences in callback between Arabic-names and North African-named applicants, but for both minority groups, male applicants received far fewer callbacks than female applicants (for reviews of field experiments of employment discrimination, see Riach and Rich 2002; Rich 2014; Zschirnt and Ruedin 2016; Quillian et al. 2019).

While the vast majority of field experiments are conducted in the labor and housing markets, researchers have also used this method to study discrimination in other market places, such as in sales (Rich, 2014). A recent example is Bourabain and Verhaeghe's (2019) study of discrimination against women and ethnic minority customers while shopping in clothing stores in Belgium. The authors conducted an in-person audit in more than 300 shops in which men and women with Belgian and Maghrebi descent asked salesclerks for help. The study shows that customers of Maghrebi descent received unfavorable treatment in comparison to their Belgian peers when asking for help, while also experiencing fewer greetings and more surveillance by salesclerks. Further, the study demonstrates that men are significantly more greeted and approached than women within both the Maghrebi and Belgian groups and that the intensity and form of discrimination tend to be subtler and lower in high-end than in low-end stores. This example shows that researchers are able to detect subtle forms of discrimination even in market transactions not characterized by selection. However, the fact that even sales interactions play out in more or less open market arenas makes even this social domain available for researchers' experimental intervention.

All of these experimental studies have in common that they are conducted by researchers' intervention in market interactions that were naturally taking place. Indeed, the open nature of market interactions is a precondition for such studies to be executed, since it allows the researcher to assess discrimination directly without running much risk of being "caught in the act" of deception (cf., Yinger 1986). Especially when investigating discrimination in labor and housing markets by using field experiments, researchers intervene in processes that are bound to be selective. This enables "clean" estimates of discrimination against specific target groups, everything else being equal.

Although field experiments have proved important in demonstrating the prevalence of discrimination in the access to employment, housing, and product markets, research in this tradition has however seldom engaged in the broader literature on ethnic and racial discrimination, including theories aiming to explain the formation, persistence, and reproduction of inequality. Indeed, field experiment research has usually dealt with only the first set of individual-level explanations presented in Chap. 3, typically revolving around the traditional distinction between taste-based and statistical discrimination, though at times also discussing the relevance of stereotypes, organizational cultures, and sociological notions of group positioning. One explanation of why structural-level theories are regularly absent in field experiment research might be that it is hard to assess how and when structures of inequality translate into actual selection decisions. Another explanation is simply that field experiments focus on the very first stage of a market interaction – the submission of a job or housing application – and not on later forms for interaction, such as day-to-day relationships between colleagues and managers at the workplace. Indeed, the very existence of selection processes in social domains where candidates compete in an open market allows the researcher to focus mainly on the extent to which discrimination occurs, rather than on why and how racial appearance or ethnic background come to matter in these very same processes.

5.3   Discrimination Research in Systems of Equality

Research on discrimination in social domains characterized by systems of equality, such as schools, health care, and public services, stands in contrast to the above-mentioned studies. Most importantly, research on discrimination in such domains are almost exclusively based on indirect measures, either by assessing ethnic inequalities at the aggregate level by the use of the residual method, or by studying more subtle acts of discrimination by the use of qualitative approaches, such as in-depth interviews and participatory observation. In both cases, the measure of discrimination is less clear-cut than the differential treatment of otherwise similar individuals found in experimental studies. However, the in-depth study of discrimination, which is especially found in qualitative approaches, has other important merits, such as the ability to analyze the findings in light of theoretical frameworks based on broader structures of inequality. Both in terms of methods and theories and the forms of discrimination detected, studies of discrimination in systems of equality consequently differ from studies of discrimination in systems of differentiation.

A typical example of this research tradition is Çelik's (2015) study among male second-generation Turkish students in Germany. The students were participating in a vocational preparation program offered by the public labor office, and Çelik bases his study on a combination of semi-structured in-depth interviews and 6 months of participatory observation of everyday life in school. Although the interviewed individuals vary greatly in their general perceptions and opinions, they all had a strong sense of being part of a group that is systematically discriminated against, and they all had personal experiences of discrimination. The students shared a feeling that both teachers and school advisors treated them differently than majority German students and other minority students attending the same program, and that this differential treatment was due to stereotypes about young Muslim men of Turkish descent in Germany. According to Çelik, these experiences led the students to develop a reactive ethnic identity, constituted by a positive collective identity among themselves and an oppositional identity vis-à-vis majority society.

Another example is Farris and Jong's (2014) large-scale study of second-generation young women of North African and South Asian descent in Denmark, France, Italy, the Netherlands, Spain, and the UK. The study aims at disentangling the various transitions from education to work and builds on both secondary analysis of national and regional statistics and on in-depth interviews with second-generation women, ethnic community representatives, non-governmental organization (NGO) representatives, teachers, and vocational/career advisors. Employing an intersectional framework of analysis, Farris and Jong show that although there seems to be a female advantage in the educational system, career advice offices and ethnic social networks tend to channel second-generation girls toward those jobs that are "reserved" for immigrant women, such as cleaning services and care work. The authors thus argue that research on discrimination needs to acknowledge the "discontinuity" of axes of inequality, suggesting that categorical membership such as gender, race, and class come to play differently in different contexts, institutional settings, and time periods.

A final example is Hedlund and Moe's (2010) study of how indigenous people are met in the health care services in Norway. Building on in-depth interviews with Sámi women and men as well as with health and welfare professionals in rural areas where the Sámi represent a considerable minority, Hedlund and Moe demonstrate how the lack of cultural sensitivity and cultural competence among majority professionals in practice may lead to indirect discrimination of Sámi patients and clients. The Sámi in Norway, who for a long period of time were forced to assimilate into Norwegian society, maintain a strong historical memory and ties to the indigenous community. The authors argue that because these ties and memories are typically awoken in interactions with social health and welfare professionals who originates from the majority culture, the health and welfare services need to develop a cultural sensitivity to be able to provide for accommodated services and assistance for indigenous people. Interestingly, this study points to the distinction between direct and indirect discrimination, discussed in Chap. 2: In public services, treating different people as if they are similar may in practice be discriminatory. In the case of Norway, knowledge about the century-long history of structural domination of the Sámi minority is a precondition for providing adequate service and help to a population that lacks trust in the state apparatus.

These different studies show how individuals of various minority origins may experience subtle acts of discrimination in social domains characterized by systems of equality, such as schools and welfare services. The studies also demonstrate how minority individuals often interpret their experiences in light of broader structures of categorical inequality, such as being ascribed membership in Muslim or indigenous groups in Europe. Importantly, these subtle forms of discrimination detected by qualitative researchers are not readily accessible by other methods. Of course, differences in access to education or health services are detectable by statistical data, and studies using the residual method often provide strong indicators that differential treatment in systems of equality do occur (e.g., Babyar 2018; Heath and Brinbaum 2014). Qualitative studies of people's experiences, however, are necessary to explore the role discrimination plays out in micro-level processes in schools, health care, and public services. Moreover, experimental data is generally lacking in these domains, mainly because it is difficult to conduct field experiments of discrimination where intervention in a selection process is not an option. The result is that research on discrimination that occurs as part of everyday interaction in schools or in encounters between minority individuals and workers within the health and social services differs quite fundamentally from research on discrimination in social domains characterized by systems of differentiation, methodologically, theoretically, and conceptually.

5.4 Implications

Research on discrimination in systems of differentiation tends to focus empirically on the extent to which discrimination occurs in selection processes, and theoretically on whether discrimination is caused by individuals' racial animus or statistical uncertainty. Research in the system of equality, on the other hand, tends to focus on more subtle processes of stigmatization and exclusion, and it more often engages with structural-level theories of inequality. Although there exist many exceptions to this rule, in general, these two strands of research can be clearly distinguished in terms of both empirical focus and the theoretical perspectives employed. The questions are: Why is this the case – and does it matter?

The main explanation of why experimental approaches dominate research in systems of differentiation while seldom are used in systems of equality is that the modus operandi differs between domains. In domains characterized by systems of differentiation, selection processes regulate the access to goods and resources, and ultimately to power. In domains characterized by systems of equality, access to goods shall be provided to everyone who has a legitimate need for equal services. This basic distinction helps explaining why two distinct strands of discrimination research have developed, and why the dividing line between the strands not only goes between researchers' preferred choice of methods but also between the social domains in question.

Importantly, the distinction between the two different system logics has consequences for the conclusions reached by research. In systems of equality, the absence of differentiating processes in which a pool of individuals compete for scarce goods means that researchers often cannot assess the direct role of discrimination by using field experiments. As field experiments are considered the gold standard in discrimination research, this implies that research cannot provide "clear and convincing evidence" (cf., Fix and Struyk 1993) of discrimination in systems of equality. By implication, conclusions drawn by research in systems of equality are deemed "uncertain" because – as shown in Chap. 4 – other methods suffer from limitations when the task is to investigate the prevalence of discrimination.

The reverse problem exists in systems of differentiation. Because researchers do have access to selection processes it is a relatively easy task to detect discrimination by conducting field experiments, thereby assessing the extent to which discrimination takes place. However, although selection regulates access to social domains such as the labor market and the housing market, these social domains – and especially the labor market – also consist of a range of everyday encounters, for example between colleagues at the workplace. Of course, discrimination may take place in these encounters too and there exists a large literature on workplace bias (e.g., Bielby 2008; Brief 2008; Wrench 2007). Yet because these interactions are not readily available for experimental intervention, research on subtle acts of discrimination in the workplace is far less prevalent than research on discrimination in the access to the labor market.

Because different methods provide different information about the type of discrimination that occurs, it is difficult to compare the extent of discrimination across social domains. This point brings us back to Reskin's (2012) observation, namely that there is a lack of studies which investigate patterns of disadvantage across different areas of social life and how disadvantage may cumulate over time and space (see also Blank et al. 2004; and this book's Chaps. 2 and 3). One reason why such studies are so rare is the fact that while discrimination is easily detected in social domains characterized by systems of differentiation, it is harder to uncover the discrimination that de facto occurs in social domains characterized by systems of equality.

References

Auspurg, K., Schneck, A., & Hinz, T. (2019). Closed doors everywhere? A meta-analysis of field experiments on ethnic discrimination in rental housing markets. *Journal of Ethnic and Migration Studies, 45*(1), 95–114. https://doi.org/10.1080/1369183X.2018.1489223.

Babyar, J. (2018). Equitable health: Let's stick together as we address global discrimination, prejudice, and stigma. *Archives of Public Health, 76*, 44–44. https://doi.org/10.1186/s13690-018-0291-3.

Baldini, M., & Federici, M. (2011). Ethnic discrimination in the Italian rental housing market. *Journal of Housing Economics, 20*, 1–14. https://doi.org/10.1016/j.jhe.2011.02.003.

Bielby, W. T. (2008). Promoting racial diversity at work: Challenges and solutions. In A. Brief (Ed.), *Diversity at work* (pp. 53–86). Cambridge, MA: Cambridge University Press.

Blank, R. M., Dabady, M., & Citro, C. F. (Eds.). (2004). *Measuring racial discrimination. Panel on methods for assessing discrimination.* Washington, DC: National Research Council, National Academies Press.

Bourabain, D., & Verhaeghe, P.-P. (2019). Could you help me, please? Intersectional field experiments on everyday discrimination in clothing stores. *Journal of Ethnic and Migration Studies, 45*(11), 2026–2044. https://doi.org/10.1080/1369183X.2018.1480360.

Brief, A. (Ed.). (2008). *Diversity at work.* Cambridge, MA: Cambridge University Press.

Bursell, M. (2014). The multiple burdens of foreign-named men—Evidence from a field experiment on gendered ethnic hiring discrimination in Sweden. *European Sociological Review, 30*(3), 399–409. https://doi.org/10.1093/esr/jcu047.

Çelik, Ç. (2015). 'Having a German passport will not make me German': Reactive ethnicity and oppositional identity among disadvantaged male Turkish second-generation youth in Germany. *Ethnic and Racial Studies, 38*(9), 1646–1662. https://doi.org/10.1080/01419870.2015.1018298.

Farris, S. R., & Jong, S. (2014). Discontinuous intersections: Second-generation immigrant girls in transition from school to work. *Ethnic and Racial Studies, 37*(9), 1505–1525. https://doi.org/10.1080/01419870.2013.774033.

Fix, M., & Struyk, R. J. (Eds.). (1993). *Clear and convincing evidence: Measurement of discrimination in America.* Washington, DC: The Urban Institute Press.

FRA. (2010). *Toward more effective policing: Understanding and preventing discriminatory ethnic profiling* (Report by European Union Agency for Fundamental Rights). Luxembourg: Publications Office of the European Union.

Goris, I., Jobard, F., & Lévy, R. (2009). Profiling minorities: *A study of stop-and-search practices in Paris.* New York: Open Society Institute.

Hedlund, M., & Moe, A. (2010). Redefining relations among minority users and social workers. *European Journal of Social Work, 13*(2), 183–198. https://doi.org/10.1080/13691451003690924.

Heath, A., & Brinbaum, Y. (2014). *Unequal attainments. Ethnic educational inequalities in ten Western countries.* Oxford: Oxford University Press.

Jobard, F., Lévy, R., Lamberth, J., Névanen, S., & Wiles-Portier, E. (2012). Measuring appearance-based discrimination: An analysis of identity checks in Paris. *Population, 67*(3), 349–375.

Quillian, L., Heath, A., Pager, D., Midtbøen, A. H., Fleischmann, F., & Hexel, O. (2019). Do some countries discriminate more than others? Evidence from 97 field experiments of racial discrimination in hiring. *Sociological Science, 6*, 467–496. https://doi.org/10.15195/v6.a18.

Reskin, B. F. (2012). The race discrimination system. *Annual Review of Sociology, 38*, 17–35. https://doi.org/10.1146/annurev-soc-071811-145508.

Riach, P., & Rich, J. (2002). Field experiments of discrimination in the market place. *The Economic Journal, 112*(483), 480–518. https://doi.org/10.1111/1468-0297.00080.

Rich, J. (2014). What do field experiments of discrimination in markets tell us? A meta-analysis of studies conducted since 2000. Bonn, *IZA Discussion Papers No. 8584.*

Staples, R. (2011). White power, black crime, and racial politics. *The Black Scholar: Journal of Black Studies and Research, 41*(4), 31–41. https://doi.org/10.5816/blackscholar.41.4.0031.

Wrench, J. (2007). *Diversity management and discrimination: Immigrants and ethnic minorities in the EU*. Aldershot: Ashgate.

Yinger, J. (1986). Measuring racial discrimination with fair housing audits: Caught in the act. *The American Economic Review, 76*(5), 881–893.

Zschirnt, E., & Ruedin, D. (2016). Ethnic discrimination in hiring decisions: A meta-analysis of correspondence tests 1990–2015. *Journal of Ethnic & Migration Studies, 42*(7), 1115–1134. https://doi.org/10.1080/1369183X.2015.1133279.

Chapter 6
Consequences of and Responses to Discrimination

After having discussed the main conceptual and methodological tools for analysis and described the forms and extent of discrimination, this chapter turns to the impact of discrimination – for economy and society, but mainly focusing on the consequences of discrimination for the targeted individuals and groups. The chapter also addresses responses to experiences of exclusion and disadvantage by reviewing recent research of how awareness of the repercussions of unfair treatment lead both individuals and groups to protect themselves and seek strategies for overcoming future barriers.

6.1 Costs of Discrimination

What is the economic costs of discrimination in the labor market? Taste-based discrimination – employers' willingness to hire a less productive employee because of ethnic or racial bias – provokes a suboptimal allocation of resources and leaves unexploited potentially valuable human resources. Theoretically, in competitive markets, such inefficient practices are likely to lower productivity and increase the risk of economic failure (Becker 1957). Because discrimination is difficult to measure directly (see Chap. 4) few empirical studies have tested this important assumption, however. A notable exception is a recent study by Pager (2016), which takes as its starting point a field experiment of discrimination in New York City, conducted in 2004. The field experiment recorded discriminatory recruitment in 24% of the tested enterprises. By matching the tested enterprises with business register data in 2010, Pager examined whether business survival during the troubled economic crisis of 2008 differed according to recruitment practices. The study shows that business failure concerned 17% of non-discriminatory firms and 36% of discriminatory companies. The findings clearly support the theoretical assumption of an association between discrimination and firm survival, as the "likelihood of going out of

R. Fibbi et al., *Migration and Discrimination*, IMISCOE Research Series,
https://doi.org/10.1007/978-3-030-67281-2_6

business for an employer who discriminated appears more than twice that of its non-discriminating counterpart" (Pager 2016: 852).

Some efforts have also been made to assess what society would gain from a reduction in discrimination. A recent French study (Bon-Maury et al. 2016), for example, aims at assessing the economic gains of eliminating discrimination in employment. The study first demonstrates considerable residual gaps in employment between men and women and French-born individuals with and without a migration background, after controlling for all available productivity-relevant factors. By simulating the effects of bringing the employment situation of discriminated persons in line with the average situation observed in the rest of the population of the same age group, the authors are able to estimate the economic gains expected from a reduction in discrimination. The study shows that a convergence in employment rates would increase the employed working population by 3% and the GDP by 3.6%.

Discriminatory practices and decisions have not only negative implications for businesses or the economy. Discrimination impacts the whole society as it may foster social exclusion by restricting full participation in the educational, economic, political, and social institutions of society. It may undermine confidence in the meritocratic system of distribution of rewards for school and professional achievement. It may jeopardize the job search process and may provoke withdrawal from the labor market which results in poverty and causes social costs due to payment of benefits. The gap between the lived reality and the expectations of equal participation may nourish frustrations and erode identification with the country and its social system. Urban residential segregation due to ethnic discrimination may further undercut minority integration. Consequently, discrimination may reinforce social inequalities in society and sharpen group cleavages and intergroup conflict, thus threatening social cohesion.

6.2   Minorities' Life Chances Reduced

Considering targeted individuals and groups, the literature on the consequences of discrimination builds on studies of experiences (see Chap. 4), which necessarily comprise different forms of unfair treatment, notably discrimination and stigmatization. Lamont et al. (2016) differentiate *discrimination* (i.e., being deprived of resources) from *stigmatization*, which refers to the experience of being disrespected, ignored, assigned a low status, or racialized. While discrimination is closely associated with stigmatization, the latter is often experienced without discrimination: incidents of stigmatization are more frequent than incidents of discrimination.

Discrimination effectively reduces a person's life chances across many domains, as aptly pointed out by Goffman (1963). It generally translates into lower attainment and unfavorable positioning for minority group members compared to the majority group. A few examples will suffice here to illustrate this point by giving a sense of the affected outcomes in education, employment, housing, life satisfaction, and health.

Discrimination in the educational field can be analyzed as the practice of individual actors. Examining the impact of teachers' expectations, Sprietsma (2013) asked primary school teachers to grade essays that had been randomly assigned to Turkish and German named pupils. The experiment reveals an ethnic bias in evaluation: the quality of the essays assigned to a Turkish name received a small yet significant 12 lower grade. The assessment of the perceived lower quality of the texts is also reflected in the teacher's secondary school recommendation for the pupil. The study thus uncovers the mechanism of the self-fulfilling prophecy, well-known as the Pygmalion effect (Rosenthal and Jacobson 1968) or its opposite, the Golem effect, which is more pertinent for the case in point.

In this social domain emblematic for "systems of equality" (see Chap. 5), alternative approaches stress the role of institutional structures and practices in generating and reproducing ethnic inequality. Gomolla and Radkte (2009) empirically backed their argument for institutional discrimination (see Chap. 3) on their study of delayed school entry for children of immigrants in comparison to children of native-born parents. Tuppat and Becker (2014) revisit these early educational disadvantages for children of immigrants, diagnosed as not ready for school. The authors compare the impact of conventional and reformed school entry procedures on delayed school entry for all children and for Turkish-origin children in a German region. The reformed method lowers the overall proportion of delayed school entry recommendation; the percentage for Turkish-origin children, although still significantly differing from majority children, reduces from 10.2 to 5.8. The authors thus demonstrate how institutional contexts shape ethnic educational inequalities already at school start.

In a somewhat similar vein, Borgna and Contini (2014) provide the most encompassing assessment of the importance of general institutional arrangements in producing social and ethnic inequalities in education. Based on the 2006–2009 waves of the Program for International Student Assessment (PISA) survey, they estimate migrant-specific penalties in educational achievement across Western European countries: "In ten countries, the average second-generation migrant child lies below the 35th percentile of the distribution of natives with the same socioeconomic resources" (Borgna and Contini 2014, 677). Cross-country migrant-specific educational achievement penalties are not explained by compositional characteristics. Late school entry and high marginalization in low-quality sectors of secondary school systems are singled out as the institutional features determining migrant-specific inequalities, distinct from those affecting class-driven educational disadvantage.

As for unemployment, the French Trajectories and Origins study shows that being a descendant of Maghrebi parents increases by six points the probability of being unemployed and decreases by five points the probability of being in full-time employment in comparison to the majority population, all other things (educational level, age, and health) being equal (Meurs 2018). To investigate the relation between perceived and actual discrimination, the author first calculates an individual indicator measuring the difference between each respondent' expected position given his personal characteristics and his actual position, providing an objective measure of the gap. By relating this indicator to perceived discrimination, she shows that what people say about their experiences of discrimination in access to employment corresponds to the "objective" measure of the injustice of their current situation.

An investigation of the rental housing market in the Flemish region reports that in almost 20% of the cases, ethnic minority members were discriminated against by not being invited to visit the property. Moreover, access to cheaper properties appear more affected by discrimination, a fact that increases housing costs for ethnic minorities at the bottom of the rental housing market (Van der Bracht et al. 2015, 172). Similarly, a Swiss study finds evidence of ethnic discrimination concerning people with Kosovar or Turkish names applying for viewing a housing accommodation: they have 3 and 5% lower response rates, respectively, than majority applicants. Whether those interested with foreign-sounding names were foreign permanent residents or Swiss citizens made hardly a difference (Auer et al. 2019).

Research has also enlarged its focus on other spheres impacted by discrimination and stigmatization. Safi's study of an encompassing dimension like life satisfaction among immigrant-origin populations in Europe starts by observing their significantly lower life satisfaction in comparison to natives (Safi 2010). Moreover, relative dissatisfaction does not diminish across time and generations; despite an average higher level of educational attainment of the younger group, the latter are more likely than their parents to consider their situation as unfair.

A vast literature analyses the relationship between discrimination and health outcomes. Discrimination is a chronic and multidimensional stressor producing harmful effects on various aspects of health: psychological and physical, as well as on health-related behavior among minority groups. Numerous studies document the adverse impact of discrimination, both in its everyday or in its acute forms, on health. Perceived discrimination is a risk factor (e.g., for cardiovascular disease) among African American men as well as for breast cancer young black women in the US (DeLilly and Flaskerud 2012). Risk factors linked to perceived racial discrimination affect health even after controlling for socioeconomic status (Williams and Mohammed 2009). Recent meta-analyses (Carter et al. 2017; Paradies et al. 2015; Pascoe and Smart Richman 2009) indicate that exposure to discrimination seems to have a stronger effect for mental health compared with physical health: it generates depression and anxiety as responses to severe stress among stigmatized, racial, and immigrant groups. Greater racial discrimination is associated with greater psychological distress. Racial discrimination has also a negative impact on cultural variables such as collective self-esteem and identity, compromising individuals' sense of self and group-based identity. Men are more affected by racial discrimination than women are (Carter et al. 2017).

In Europe, this new strand of research investigating the impact of discrimination on health is best established in the UK. To determine the causal link between the two variables, Johnston and Lordan's (2012), for example, study the health records of Pakistanis and Bangladeshis before and after the September 11th, 2001 attacks, which caused a sharp increase of anti-Muslim discrimination in the UK. The health indicators of these groups are compared to the ones of the control group, non-Muslim Indians. Analyzing changes in health indicators between 1999 and 2004, the authors evaluate the worsening of the general health of Muslim Pakistanis and Bangladeshis relative to the general health of the control group, concluding that "he probability of bad or very bad health increased by 3.0 percentage points, and the probability of poor health limiting normal activities increased by 5.2 percentage points." (2012, 15). Johnston and Lordan further assess that discrimination exerts an indirect detrimental impact on health, by negatively affecting notably employment and perceived social support and by reducing health-related behaviors.

Moreover, perceived discrimination is negatively associated with health care service utilization, concludes another meta-analysis (Ben et al. 2017). Those who experienced discrimination have 2 or 3 times higher probability of reporting lower trust in healthcare systems, lower level of satisfaction with health services and lower quality of communication with healthcare professionals. Experiences of discrimination also increase the risks of delayed care and of non-compliance with the recommended treatment.

Most studies analyze the relation between perceived interpersonal discrimination and health while there is a lack of studies exploring the link between structural discrimination and health inequalities (Krieger 2014). Yet recent research (Paradies et al. 2015) investigates the impact of cumulative discrimination and institutional racism (see Chap. 3) on health outcomes by taking into consideration the larger environment in the belief that health equity is influenced by the place where people live and work. Sociological research emphasizes residential segregation as the key institutional mechanism and fundamental cause of health disparities (Massey 2004). The neighborhood is a critical factor mediating access to social, economic, and human capital, reflected in the strong association between segregation and poverty (Wilson 1987). The theoretical explanation of the link between segregation and detrimental outcomes in educational achievement, employment, incarceration, and welfare dependency rests on social mechanisms like peer influences, cultural diffusion, role models, and access to networks. This literature thus echoes the environmental explanation of health disparities advanced at the end of the nineteenth century by W. E. B. Du Bois (1899).

6.3 Responses to Discrimination and Stigmatization

Discrimination and stigmatization affect the life chances of the targeted persons and groups and are a source of stress affecting their well-being. Yet individuals and groups that are victims of discrimination react by elaborating response strategies. The step from discriminatory experiences and response strategies is filtered by the way those experiences are lived and unraveled. Perception is driven by the actual existence of inequality: those who are disadvantaged are usually likely to feel discrimination. For instance, visible minorities who experience greater disadvantages also perceive more discrimination than their majority counterparts do (Andriessen et al. 2014). Yet appraisal is a matter of interpretation attributing (e.g., a negative outcome in the labor market) to lack of personal skills or ascribing it to the targeted group's prejudice and unfair treatment. Individual differences impinge upon the perception of discrimination. Therefore, long-term immigrants in Canada are more likely to perceive discrimination than new immigrants (Banerjee 2008). Similarly, as children of immigrants have larger opportunities of establishing equal contact with majority members than first-generation immigrants, they may perceive less discrimination (André and Dronkers 2017). However, better-educated children of immigrants tend to have an enhanced awareness of discrimination in comparison to the previous migrant generation (Borrell et al. 2015), because of higher expectations for fair treatment. International evidence assesses "that more discrimination is found in the lower segments of the labor market" (Andriessen et al. 2012, 256; Carlsson 2010) so that higher educated minority members appear less exposed to discrimination than lower educated ones. Nevertheless, perceived discrimination seem to be higher among better-educated immigrant minority members (Diehl and Liebau 2017; De Vroome et al. 2014): this "paradox of integration" is partially explained by a heightened sense of relative deprivation; that is, the feeling of being illegitimately disadvantaged in comparison to majority members (Steinmann 2018). Moreover, ethnic identification is positively associated with perceived racial discrimination (Sellers and Shelton 2003; Verkuyten 2005).

Many studies assess that respondents perceive a higher level of discrimination directed at their in-group than at themselves as members of that group. This discrepancy may be due to the difficulty of detecting discrimination as the source of personal disadvantage in individual cases, in comparison to reliance on public measures of discrimination at the group level. On the other hand, exaggerating discrimination at the group level can be used as a claim argument for promoting the improvement of the minority group.

Furthermore, perception of discrimination is driven by targeted people's awareness of their rights and their sensitivity to unfair treatment, therefore it depends also on the prevailing social norms in a certain place and point in time. The establishment of equality norms increases the perception of discrimination: a treatment that used to be accepted as normal may be (re)qualified as unfair and become untenable. In a recent meta-analysis of US studies on the impact of workplace discrimination, Triana et al. (2015) find that the well-documented negative relation between perceived ethnic discrimination and job attitudes (e.g., withdrawals, efforts, etc.) was stronger after the adoption of the Civil Rights Act of 1991, reflecting a keen demand for fair treatment and implementing a stronger commitment to equality.

Perceiving discrimination, individuals and groups react to it in order to maintain self-esteem, a sense of control over the world around them and to seek ways out of the deadlock. They can act on the present, weigh up the alternatives in order to achieve the desired outcomes and project themselves into the future (Bandura 2001, 2006). The range of reactions and responses may differ in many regards, according to the actor's level, to the perception of the stressing factor, to the types of action and/or reflection, to the aim pursued by the response, as well as to the socio-historical and cultural context.

6.3.1 Coping and Identity Strategies

Individual-level responses to interpersonal forms of discrimination and stigmatization may be subsumed under the general concept of coping. Coping is stress-buffering answers aiming at reducing the effects of discrimination and stigmatization (Brondolo et al. 2009), notably on mental and physical health. Murray and Ali (2017) provide examples of such responses in a qualitative study on how senior professional Muslim women in the UK and Australia live, adapt, and react to discrimination in the workplace. They find two kinds of responses: the first type aims at modifying the source of stress and seeking social support (problem-focused coping) while the second one aims at reducing the distress associated with stigmatization (emotion-focused coping; see also Folkman and Lazarus 1984). Responses tend to vary according to the way the stress is perceived: when individuals see the situation as a challenge, they tend to resort to active problem-solving responses, like discussing concerns openly or referring to a supervisor. When they perceive the stress as a threat, they seek protection in emotion-focused responses, like learning to accommodate the values of their host society or looking for comfort in religion by seeking God's help. Actions take place largely on an individual level, while support from groups is sought in situations deemed threatening. Testing the buffering effects of coping responses among black women, Krieger (1990) finds that those who take a problem-solving approach are less likely to have a hypertension diagnosis than those who take an emotion-focused coping response.

A large body of literature focuses on the impact of discrimination and stigmatization on social identity. Since people have the general desire to establish a positive social identity, a disadvantaged in-group targeted by discrimination results in a negative social identity (Tajfel and Turner 1979). To pursue status improvement despite this unsatisfactory situation, minority members anticipating discrimination may respond individually or as a group. The choice among strategies rests on an evaluation of their feasibility. If group boundaries are deemed permeable, then members of minority groups will attempt to enhance their identity by "walking out" of their in-group and by identifying with and joining the majority group. Indeed, Hirschman (1970) names this strategy "exit," when applying it at a macro systemic level of analysis. Moreover, assimilation can be considered as a strategy to enhance individual position (Berry 1984).

Studies on labor market discrimination pinpoint minority job seekers' strategies to enhance individual chances to gain access to the workplace. In Sweden, taking advantage of institutionally provided support facilitating such response, minority job seekers adopt a Swedish-sounding name in public, while retaining their ethnic name and identity in the private sphere (Bursell 2012). Similarly, according to Kang et al. (2016), African and Asian-American students often "whitewash" their résumés by concealing their origin when applying for work. In order to be seen as a member of the dominant group, they present themselves omitting their minority-sounding first name or using an additional majority-sounding name or spending their middle name. Another way of whitening job applications is limiting information on aspects of one's curriculum that might be the basis for stigmatization. Applicants will then omit some engagements or modify the account of their involvement in ethnic experiences or mention "white" activities to show an assimilated profile. Concealing and downplaying their stigmatized identity strongly remind of Goffman's strategies of "passing" and "covering" for the management of stigmatized identities (Goffman 1963). Whitening a résumé proves an effective strategy: it generally enhances callbacks in comparison to unwhitened applications and nearly doubles the callback rate for Asian applicants in Kang et al.'s (2016) correspondence test. Such individual mobility strategy allows successful members of a minority group who pursue their career while the status relations between majority and minority remain unchanged.

Sonia Kang et al.'s study "Whitened Résumés: Race and Self-Presentation in the Labor Market", published in *Administrative Science Quarterly* in 2016, is a prime example of how racialized minorities may act when anticipating discrimination. It is also an innovative study, methodologically speaking: Combining qualitative interviews, a laboratory experiment and a field experiment, the authors examine racial minorities' attempts to avoid discrimination in labor markets by concealing or downplaying racial cues in job applications, a practice they refer to as "résumé whitening." Besides documenting that résumé whitening is a widespread practice which increases the possibilities of receiving call-backs for job interviews, the study shows that minorities are less inclined to "whitewash" their CVs when confronted with employers that present themselves as pro-diversity. However, the field experiment suggests that organizational diversity statements are not associated with reduced discrimination against unwhitened, leading to the paradoxical conclusion that minorities may be particularly likely to experience disadvantage when they apply to allegedly pro-diversity employers.

In contrast, if barriers between groups are perceived as insurmountable, individual strategies prove impracticable. Persons targeted by stigmatization and discrimination may, therefore, resort to collective responses: in an attempt to improve their position, they might seek to modify the relations between majority and minority. Collective responses build on the recognition of one's membership in the group and on a compelling identification to the in-group. Increased identification with the in-group aims at protecting psychological well-being (Branscombe et al. 1999). Having a strong relation to one's ethnic group identity may moderate the stress of discrimination by preventing negative stereotypes from affecting the self-concept. This rejection-identification model is corroborated by numerous empirical studies

(Schmitt et al. 2014). In research among young Turkish-Dutch and Dutch persons of similar educational backgrounds in the Netherlands, Verkuyten (2008), for example, observes that the higher the perceived discrimination among Turkish-Dutch, the stronger their Turkish group identification. In turn, this enhances their psychological well-being, partly restoring the damage inflicted by the discrimination.

Moreover, when the disadvantaged position is deemed illegitimate, it may give rise to a feeling of injustice and dissatisfaction. Collective mobilization is mostly based on relative deprivation, that is, the subjective perception of disadvantage and its illegitimate character rather than on the objective circumstances (Walker and Smith 2002). Collective mobilization is more likely to occur when a window of opportunity arises. The 1983 French March for Equality and Against Racism is an example in this regard. The March from Marseille to Paris, often known as "Marche des Beurs," was a reaction against stigmatization and racial inequalities faced by children of Maghrebi immigrants, after the 1981 election of the first socialist president, François Mitterrand, which had stirred high expectations. French second-generation individuals mobilized as an actor in a social movement calling for equal rights based on the recognition of their French citizenship. This movement's attempt to modify their unsatisfactory situation illustrates the "voice" option, among the famous triad of strategies outlined by Hirschman (1970).

6.3.2 Reactive Ethnicity

In the sociology of integration literature, the link between disadvantaged positions and ethnic group identification is often understood as an expression of the immigrant population's alleged limited willingness to integrate (Heath 2014), raising anxiety among majority group members. This common assumption in public debates disregards the well-established relation between perceived discrimination and a response strategy of stigmatized groups to protect their well-being, known in the literature on second-generation incorporation as "reactive ethnicity." When confronted with a hostile reception environment, children of immigrants develop a defensive identity reactivating their origin, in order to reinforce the collective worth of their in-group (Portes and Rumbaut 2001).

Qualitative studies deliver penetrating insights into the logics of such identification reactions. Mey and Rorato (2010), for example, interviewed children of immigrants in Switzerland before and after their transition from compulsory school to vocational training. They document how those youngsters who repeatedly fail in their efforts to find an apprenticeship increasingly develop a strong identification with their origin group. Çelik's (2015) previously cited study among Turkish school dropouts in their vocational preparation program in Germany points in a similar direction. Observing their teachers' differential treatment of pupils, Çelik shows that the students in his study develop a deep sense of discrimination targeting especially groups singularized along ethnic and religious boundaries, like Turks, Kurds, and Arabs in contrast with other immigrants of Christian background (see Chap. 5). Far from displaying a hyphenated identity, the informants exhibit a strong commitment to their Turkish identity as a response to their experience of discrimination and their perception of blocked social mobility. Çelik argues that when perceived discrimination is linked to stigmatization (i.e., rejection of the minority culture by the majority group), reactive ethnicity turns into the adoption of an oppositional identity (see also Ogbu 1991). Minorities refuse symbols and behaviors of the majority, discredited as a form of "acting white" and develop an "alternative cultural frame of reference" (i.e., different antithetical values to the dominant culture).

6.3.3   Socio-Cultural Embedding of Minority Responses

While in most studies, analyses are confined to one single national context, the comparative and multilevel research by Lamont and her colleagues (2016) allows for an exploration of the variability of subjective interpretations and the responses to perceived stigmatization in relation to the historical and social context. The authors analyze how middle- and working-class African Americans in the US, black Brazilians in Brazil, and Arab Palestinians in Israel interpret the discrimination and stigmatization they experience. They develop a five-category classification of narratives of incidents as well as of actual and normative responses. The most frequent responses are confronting the stigmatizer (i.e., challenging the perpetrator); managing the self (i.e., weighing the personal costs of responding) and not responding (i.e., regularly avoiding responding). Less common responses are focusing on hard work and competency (i.e. acquiring credentials and credit) and engaging in the group's isolation.

Lamont et al.'s (2016) comparative analysis reveals interesting cross-country differences. While African Americans predominantly react on discrimination by confrontation, black Brazilians hesitate between confronting, managing the self, and non-responding. Arab Palestinians, by contrast, opt most often for ignoring their experiences and retreating in isolation. The authors explain those cross-country variations by referring to the cultural repertoires available in each specific national context. Such repertoires are "cultural frames they [minorities] mobilize to make sense of their experience and to determine how to respond" (Lamont and Mizrachi 2012, 365). The ways minorities live and interpret their situations in each country are shaped by the historical place of the group in the country (past slavery and today's racism in American society, the myth of racial democracy in Brazil, and the Zionist national ideology in Israel), by institutional dimensions (e.g., the legal culture built on the Civil Rights Acts in the US and the legal and spatial segregation in Israel) and finally by the strength of a perceived minority group identity. Those features represent enabling and constraining forces that shape the actions of individuals and groups when addressing stigmatization.

6.4 Conclusion

Discrimination and stigmatization are costly for the society by lowering economic growth, by reinforcing ethnic inequalities, by fueling political conflicts and by jeopardizing social cohesion. Moreover, victims of unfair treatment pay a high price as discrimination and stigmatization reproduce the privilege of the majority, perpetuate their own disadvantaged status by eroding their life's chances in many social domains. Far from being passive victims, however, many members of minority groups develop and deploy individual and collective strategies to meet such challenges. Responses vary according to their perception of the discrimination, the resources they can activate in their struggle, their evaluation of the chance to change their inequitable condition, and the rhetorical and strategic tools they can mobilize.

References

André, S., & Dronkers, J. (2017). Perceived in-group discrimination by first- and second-generation immigrants from different countries of origin in 27 EU member-states. *International Sociology, 32*(1), 105–129.

Andriessen, I., Nievers, E., Dagevos, J., & Faulk, L. (2012). Ethnic discrimination in the Dutch labor market: Its relationship with job characteristics and multiple group membership. *Work and Occupations, 39*(3), 237–269. https://doi.org/10.1177/0730888412444783.

Andriessen, I., Fernee, H., & Wittebrood, K. (2014). *Perceived discrimination in the Netherlands.* Den Haag: Netherlands Institute for Social Research (SCP).

Auer, D., Lacroix, J., Ruedin, D., & Zschirnt, E. (2019). *Ethnische Diskriminierung auf dem Schweizer Wohnungsmarkt.* Grenchen: Bundesamt für Wohnungswesen.

Bandura, A. (2001). Social cognitive theory: An agentic perspective. *Annual Review of Psychology, 52*(1), 1–26.

Bandura, A. (2006). Toward a psychology of human agency. *Perspectives on Psychological Science, 1*(2), 164–180. https://doi.org/10.1111/j.1745-6916.2006.00011.x.

Banerjee, R. (2008). An examination of factors affecting perception of workplace discrimination. *Journal of Labor Research, 29*(4), 380. https://doi.org/10.1007/s12122-008-9047-0.

Becker, G. S. (1957). *The economics of discrimination.* Chicago: Chicago University Press.

Ben, J., Cormack, D., Harris, R., & Paradies, Y. (2017). Racism and health service utilisation: A systematic review and meta-analysis. *PLoS One, 12*(12), e0189900.

Berry, J. W. (1984). Cultural relations in plural societies: Alternatives to segregation and their sociopsychological implications. In N. Miller, B. Marilynn, & I. Brewer (Eds.), *Groups in contact.* New York: Academic.

Bon-Maury, G., Bruneau, C., Dherbécourt, C., Diallo, A., Flamand, J., Gilles, C., & Trannoy, A. (2016). *Le coût économique des discriminations.* Rapport à la ministre du Travail, de l'Emploi, de la Formation professionnelle et du Dialogue social, et au ministre de la Ville, de la Jeunesse et des Sports. Paris: France Stratégie.

Borgna, C., & Contini, D. (2014). Migrant achievement penalties in Western Europe: Do educational systems matter? *European Sociological Review, 30*(5), 670–683. https://doi.org/10.1093/esr/jcu067.

Borrell, C., Palència, L., Bartoll, X., Ikram, U., & Malmusi, D. (2015). Perceived discrimination and health among immigrants in Europe according to national integration policies. *International Journal of Environmental Research and Public Health, 12*(9), 10687–10699.

Branscombe, N. R., Schmitt, M. T., & Harvey, R. D. (1999). Perceiving pervasive discrimination among African Americans: Implications for group identification and well-being. *Journal of Personality and Social Psychology, 77*(1), 135.

Brondolo, E., Ver Halen, N. B., Pencille, M., Beatty, D., & Contrada, R. J. (2009). Coping with racism: A selective review of the literature and a theoretical and methodological critique. *Journal of Behavioral Medicine, 32*(1), 64–88. https://doi.org/10.1007/s10865-008-9193-0.

Bursell, M. (2012). Name change and Destigmatization among middle eastern immigrants in Sweden. *Ethnic and Racial Studies, 35*(3), 471–487. https://doi.org/10.1080/0141987 0.2011.589522.

Carlsson, M. (2010). Experimental evidence of discrimination in the hiring of first- and second-generation immigrants. *Labour, 24*(3), 263–278. https://doi.org/10.1111/j.1467-9914.2010. 00482.x.

Carter, R. T., Lau, M. Y., Johnson, V., & Kirkinis, K. (2017). Racial discrimination and health outcomes among racial/ethnic minorities: A meta-analytic review. *Journal of Multicultural Counseling and Development, 45*(4), 232–259. https://doi.org/10.1002/jmcd.12076.

Çelik, Ç. (2015). 'Having a German passport will not make me German': Reactive ethnicity and oppositional identity among disadvantaged male Turkish second-generation youth in Germany. *Ethnic and Racial Studies, 38*(9), 1646–1662. https://doi.org/10.1080/01419870.201 5.1018298.

De Vroome, T., Martinovic, B., & Verkuyten, M. (2014). The integration paradox: Level of education and immigrants' attitudes toward natives and the host society. *Cultural Diversity and Ethnic Minority Psychology, 20*(2), 166. https://doi.org/10.1037/a0034946.

DeLilly, C. R., & Flaskerud, J. H. (2012). Discrimination and health outcomes. *Issues in Mental Health Nursing, 33*(11), 801–804. https://doi.org/10.3109/01612840.2012.671442.

Diehl, C., & Liebau, E. (2017). Perceptions of discrimination: What do they measure and why do they matter? *SOEPpapers No. 945.*

Du Bois, W. E. B. (1899). *The Philadelphia negro: A social study.* Philadelphia, PA: University of Pennsylvania.

Folkman, S., & Lazarus, R. S. (1984). *Stress, appraisal, and coping.* New York: Springer.

Goffman, E. (1963). *Stigma: Notes on the management of spoiled identity.* Englewood Cliffs: Prentice-Hall.

Gomolla, M., & Radtke, F.-O. (2009). *Institutionelle Diskriminierung: die Herstellung ethnischer Differenz in der Schule.* Wiesbaden: Springer VS.

Heath, A. (2014). Introduction: Patterns of generational change: Convergent, reactive, or emergent? *Ethnic and Racial Studies, 37*(1), 1–9. https://doi.org/10.1080/01419870.2014.844845.

Hirschman, A. O. (1970). *Exit, voice, and loyalty. Responses to decline in firms, organizations, and states.* Cambridge: Harvard University Press.

Johnston, D. W., & Lordan, G. (2012). Discrimination makes me sick! An examination of the discrimination-health relationship. *Journal of Health Economics, 31*(1), 99–111. https://doi. org/10.1016/j.jhealeco.2011.12.002.

Kang, S. K., DeCelles, K. A., Tilcsik, A., & Jun, S. (2016). Whitened resumes: Race and self-presentation in the labor market. *Administrative Science Quarterly, 61*(3), 469–502. https://doi. org/10.1177/0001839216639577.

Krieger, N. (1990). Racial and gender discrimination: Risk factors for high blood pressure? *Social Science & Medicine, 30*(12), 1273–1281. https://doi.org/10.1016/0277-9536(90)90307-E.

Krieger, N. (2014). Discrimination and health inequities. *International Journal of Health Services, 44*(4), 643–710. https://doi.org/10.2190/HS.44.4.b.

Lamont, M., & Mizrachi, N. (2012). Ordinary people doing extraordinary things: Responses to stigmatization in comparative perspective. *Ethnic and Racial Studies, 35*(3), 365–381. https:// doi.org/10.1080/01419870.2011.589528.

Lamont, M., Silva, G. M., Welburn, J., Guetzkow, J., Mizrachi, N., Herzog, H., & Reis, E. (2016). *Getting respect: Responding to stigma and discrimination in the United States, Brazil, and Israel.* Princeton, NJ: Princeton University Press.

Massey, D. S. (2004). Segregation and stratification: A biosocial perspective. *Du Bois Review: Social Science Research on Race, 1*(1), 7–25. https://doi.org/10.1017/S1742058X04040032.

Meurs, D. (2018). Employment and wages of immigrants and descendants of immigrants: Measures of inequality and perceived discrimination. In C. Beauchemin, C. Hamel, & P. Simon (Eds.), *Trajectories and origins: Survey on the diversity of the French population* (pp. 78–106). Cham: Springer.

Mey, E., & Rorato, M. (2010). *Jugendliche mit Migrationshintergrund im Übergang ins Erwachsenenalter – eine biographische Längsschnittstudie.* Luzern: Hochschule Luzern – Soziale Arbeit.

Murray, P. A., & Ali, F. (2017). Agency and coping strategies for ethnic and gendered minorities at work. *The International Journal of Human Resource Management, 28*(8), 1236–1260. https://doi.org/10.1080/09585192.2016.1166787.

Ogbu, J. U. (1991). Immigrant and involuntary minorities in comparative perspective. In M. A. Gibson & J. U. Ogbu (Eds.), *In Minority status and schooling.* New York: Garland.

Pager, D. (2016). Are firms that discriminate more likely to go out of business? *Sociological Science, 3*, 849–859. https://doi.org/10.15195/v3.a36.

Paradies, Y., Ben, J., Denson, N., Elias, A., Priest, N., Pieterse, A., Gupta, A., Kelaher, M., & Gee, G. (2015). Racism as a determinant of health: A systematic review and meta-analysis. *PLoS One, 10*(9), e0138511. https://doi.org/10.1371/journal.pone.0138511.

Pascoe, E. A., & Smart Richman, L. (2009). Perceived discrimination and health: A meta-analytic review. *Psychological Bulletin, 135*(4), 531. https://doi.org/10.1037/a0016059.

Portes, A., & Rumbaut, R. (Eds.). (2001). *Legacies: The story of the immigrant second generation.* Los Angeles: University of California Press.

Rosenthal, R., & Jacobson, L. (1968). *Pygmalion in the classroom.* New York: Holt, Rinehart, and Winston.

Safi, M. (2010). Immigrants' life satisfaction in Europe: Between assimilation and discrimination. *European Sociological Review, 26*(2), 159–176. https://doi.org/10.1093/esr/jcp013.

Schmitt, M. T., Branscombe, N. R., Postmes, T., & Garcia, A. (2014). The consequences of perceived discrimination for psychological Well-being: A meta-analytic review. *Psychological Bulletin, 140*(4), 921. https://doi.org/10.1037/a0035754.

Sellers, R. M., & Shelton, J. N. (2003). The role of racial identity in perceived racial discrimination. *Journal of Personality and Social Psychology, 84*(5), 1079. https://doi.org/10.1037/0022-3514.84.5.1079.

Sprietsma, M. (2013). Discrimination in grading: Experimental evidence from primary school teachers. *Empirical Economics, 45*(1), 523–538. https://doi.org/10.1007/s00181-012-0609-x.

Steinmann, J.-P. (2018). The paradox of integration: Why do higher educated new immigrants perceive more discrimination in Germany? *Journal of Ethnic and Migration Studies*, 1–24. https://doi.org/10.1080/1369183X.2018.1480359.

Tajfel, H., & Turner, J. C. (1979). An integrative theory of intergroup conflict. In W. G. Austin & S. Worchel (Eds.), *The social psychology of intergroup relations* (pp. 33–47). Belmont, CA: Nelson-Hall.

Triana, M. d. C., Jayasinghe, M., & Pieper, J. R. (2015). Perceived workplace racial discrimination and its correlates: A meta-analysis. *Journal of Organizational Behavior, 36*(4), 491–513. https://doi.org/10.1002/job.1988.

Tuppat, J., & Becker, B. (2014). Sind türkischstämmige Kinder beim Schulstart im Nachteil? *Kölner Zeitschrift für Soziologie und Sozialpsychologie, 66*(2), 219–241.

Van der Bracht, K., Coenen, A., & Van de Putte, B. (2015). The not-in-my-property syndrome: The occurrence of ethnic discrimination in the rental housing market in Belgium. *Journal of Ethnic and Migration Studies, 41*(1), 158–175. https://doi.org/10.1080/1369183X.2014.913476.

Verkuyten, M. (2005). Ethnic group identification and group evaluation among minority and majority groups: Testing the multiculturalism hypothesis. *Journal of Personality and Social Psychology, 88*(1), 121. https://doi.org/10.1037/0022-3514.88.1.121.

Verkuyten, M. (2008). Life satisfaction among ethnic minorities: The role of discrimination and group identification. *Social Indicators Research, 89*(3), 391–404.

Walker, I., & Smith, H. J. (2002). *Relative deprivation: Specification, development, and integration.* Cambridge: Cambridge University Press.

Williams, D. R., & Mohammed, S. A. (2009). Discrimination and racial disparities in health: Evidence and needed research. *Journal of Behavioral Medicine, 32*(1), 20–47. https://doi.org/10.1007/s10865-008-9185-0.

Wilson, W. J. (1987). *The truly disadvantaged.* Chicago: University of Chicago Press.

Chapter 7
Combatting Discrimination

There is a large variety of policies and actions contributing to tackling discrimination against immigrants and ethno-racial minorities. These policies can be distributed along a gradient from formal equality to proactive policies that could include preferential treatment for disadvantaged groups. Antidiscrimination laws and policies aim to prevent negative and unjustified distinction, exclusion, restriction, or preference based on grounds such as nationality, race, color, sex, language, religion, political opinion, etc. The list of grounds varies across countries: the French law, for example, identify no less than 25 criteria of discrimination, the law in countries such as Denmark or the UK operates with eight criteria, while the German General Equal Treatment Act (2006, amended 2013) mentions only six grounds. A large number of countries have chosen an open-ended list to avoid restricting the scope of discrimination.

Antidiscrimination laws and policies aim to ensure equal rights for the protected groups (e.g., women, people with disabilities, or ethnic and racial minorities). The main goal of these legal provisions, policies, and actions is to achieve equality for all in concrete terms and not only in principle. According to De Witte (2010), the common principle of equality is "broad and empty" and should be specified to become substantive. Fredman assigns four objectives to such substantive equality policies: "to redress disadvantage; to address stigma, stereotyping, prejudice and violence; to enhance voice and participation; and to accommodate difference and achieve structural change" (Fredman 2016, 713). However, while the principles and objectives of equal rights, equal treatment, and equal access to resources, goods, and services receive generally large support among policy makers and public opinion, concrete positive actions tend to be more divisive. This is especially the case of positive discrimination, which provides preferential treatment – an advantage – to members of protected groups to redress the penalties they historically have faced (and often still face), in access to higher education, political mandate, public jobs, or social housing.

Importantly, countries vary greatly in their strategies to tackle ethnic and racial discrimination. First, they can be divided into two groups: those who have adopted

© The Author(s) 2021
R. Fibbi et al., *Migration and Discrimination*, IMISCOE Research Series,
https://doi.org/10.1007/978-3-030-67281-2_7

ethnic and race-based policies, or ethnic and/or racial conscious policies, and those who favor color-blind policies, meaning that they address ethno-racial discrimination without identifying explicitly categories of victims based on ethnicity and race (see Chap. 1). Second, they diverge in the kind of measures they implement in the name of antidiscrimination policies. There are three main groups of measures – antidiscrimination legislation, affirmative action and other equal opportunity policies, and tools for promoting diversity. The chapter discusses these different measures in turn, before turning to studies that have aimed at assessing the effectiveness of measures to combat discrimination.

7.1 Antidiscrimination Legislation

Following the Universal Declaration of Human Rights, a series of international treaties and conventions promoted by the United Nations have set international norms for equality: The International Human Rights Charter, the International Covenant on Economic and Social Rights and the International Covenant on Civil and Political Rights. Principles of equality have further been detailed in thematic conventions, some of which specifically focus on racial discrimination. The International Convention on the Elimination of All Forms of Racial Discrimination adopted in 1965 and the Convention 111 of the International Labour Organization on discrimination (employment and occupation) adopted in 1958 are the main references in this area.

In Europe, the Racial Equality Directive (RED) enacted in 2000 constitutes the main legal framework on ethnic and racial discrimination. It implements the principle of equal treatment between persons irrespective of racial or ethnic origin and complements the European directives on discrimination in employment (which covers several grounds) and other directives dealing specifically with gender, age, disability, religion, or sexual orientation. The RED came relatively late after the pioneering antidiscrimination law implemented by the UK in 1976, which served as a reference for the European Commission. Similar legislation can be found in immigration countries at much earlier dates – such as Australia's Racial Discrimination Act of 1975, the Canadian Human Rights Act of 1977, and Title VII of the Civil Rights Act in the US enacted in 1964 (Simon 2005).

Each antidiscrimination law provides for the creation of agencies responsible for monitoring its application and for implementing its programs. At the inception of the process, agencies tend to be specialized on a specific ground (gender, race and ethnicity, disability), but the recent trend is to merge these together into a single body. For example, the British Commission for Racial Equality, the Equal Opportunity Commission, and the Disability Rights Commission were grouped together in the Equality and Human Rights Commission, established by the Equality Act of 2006. The creation of an independent equality body is a requirement spelled out in the RED, and all EU member countries have more or less complied with this. In addition to the national equality bodies, the European Commission established the EU Agency for Fundamental Rights (FRA) in 2007, as well as a network of equality bodies, called EQUINET, created in 2002–2004. However, even in the common framework provided by the EU directives, antidiscrimination actions vary greatly among EU countries. The prerogatives of these agencies in combatting discrimination can be far-reaching, ranging from the awareness raising of public authorities and civil society to the coordination of equality policies. They are responsible for all complaint-handling activities and may conduct legal actions and investigations.

Antidiscrimination laws can be enforced in civil, administrative, or criminal courts. There are important differences in these legal tracks in terms of plaintiffs, procedures, and sanctions or sentencing. However, enforcement of the law can take non-judicial procedures aside from these judicial proceedings: negotiation or mediation can be actively promoted by equality bodies that are not judicial entities. In addition, labor inspectorates are often charged to enforce the employment law and its provision on discrimination.

The legal context itself produces large disparities in the outcome of the legal actions, and differences in organizational structures have an impact on the efficiency of the legal antidiscrimination framework. Comparative studies on the implementation of antidiscrimination laws have shown significant variations across European countries when it comes to access to rights and the efficiency of legal action. For example, shifting the burden of proof – meaning that the defendant (e.g., the employer) has to prove that the treatment was not discriminatory – is not available in all EU countries, and in those where the provision exists, not in all judicial procedures. Protections against victimization of plaintiffs in retaliation of their claim are inconsistent in some countries, and lack credibility in others. Sanctions and remedies differ greatly in their capacity to punish and prevent discrimination acts, reflecting the different concepts of equality and the legal order governing each national context. Even under the EU antidiscrimination law, no comprehensive system has been adopted so far.

Equality bodies are generally entitled to receive complaints, to assist victims in litigations and sometimes have the legal power to take sanctions and make legal decisions. Negotiation, mediation, or conciliation are often preferred to litigation since discrimination cases often proved to be difficult to prosecute in the courts. Equality bodies have frequently prioritized strategic litigation whereas a limited number of cases are selected to set changes in court practices. Filing a complaint in court might be complicated in some countries, and the outcome of these complaints are rarely successful (FRA 2012). A gap between complaints and lawsuits can be observed in France where the former equality body (HALDE) treated 5658 files of complaints in 2010, of which 127 legal cases were completed (in various categories). In less than a handful of cases, condemnations actually took place, although a large number of files had been treated through mediation. In general, legal action against ethnic and racial discrimination is less developed than against sex or disability discrimination. For example, in England and Wales in 2019, the Employment Tribunal has treated 9427 complaints of sex discrimination, 6919 for disability, 3589 for race, and 753 for religion. In addition, 27,730 cases came under the equal pay law, which is a sub-type of sex discrimination. Although legal prosecution is an important part of antidiscrimination action, the legal framework has to be complemented by policies and more proactive strategies to control practices and processes without waiting for a complaint to be filed in.

7.2 Antidiscrimination Policies: Positive Action

Despite the difference in wording, affirmative action and positive action are essentially the same kinds of policies. The former concept originated in the US, while the latter, inspired by the UK, was adopted by the European action plan against discrimination (McCrudden 1986). As Daniel Sabbagh summarizes it, the goal of such positive action "is to counter deeply entrenched social practices that reproduce group-structured inequality (even in the absence of intentional discrimination) by creating positive externalities beyond individual recipients" (Sabbagh 2011, 109). Still, there exists a variety of measures in positive action policies that differentiate them along a continuum of the transformative powers of the actions.

7.2.1 Awareness Raising

All antidiscrimination policies begin with awareness raising through communication campaigns. The objective is to disseminate the framing in terms of discrimination to create consciousness among victims and potential authors. Indeed, the capacity to tackle discrimination depends on the conceptualization of the phenomenon, as well as the underlying understanding of how it operates and what consequences it causes for disadvantaged groups. There are different ways to address biases and inequalities generated by discrimination, beginning with programs to empower underrepresented minorities, actions to pursue a higher level of impartiality in decision-making by acting directly on processes and developing training and eventually schemes to impose preferential treatment for certain categories of disadvantaged groups, including quota systems. In the following, we detail some of these actions with examples from practices in different countries. Although there are trends of cross-national harmonization of legal frameworks, antidiscrimination policies tend to remain country-specific. What applies to one country might not be available in another one, even in Europe where the European Commission has stimulated the adoption of common legal and practical tools.

7.2.2 Outreach Programs

One way to increase participation in the education or labor markets is to develop information about opportunities to underrepresented ethnic and racial minorities. These programs are called "outreach" because they target specific population groups or places that are usually not reached by information about the existence of opportunities. The rationale behind these programs is that minorities do not consider applying to selective tracks in education or advantageous job positions because they do not feel entitled to it or do not have access to the relevant information. Outreach programs are frequent in education to attract minority students in selective programs where they tend to be highly underrepresented. In France, for example, dedicated preparatory programs were developed in the 2000s to ease the access to elite schools (*grandes écoles*) for students from high schools located in disadvantaged neighborhoods (Allouch and Buisson-Fenet 2009). In employment, these schemes build on the so-called spatial mismatch theory (see Chap. 3), which suggests that minority members experience greater distance from job markets both spatially and culturally, thus attempting to compensate for this structural disadvantage by disseminating the information about job opportunities in specific locations or toward minority groups. Outreach programs aim at increasing the critical mass of minority applicants but do not address potential discrimination in selection processes.

7.2.3 Proactive Policies

One of the main goals of positive actions is to address non-intentional, systemic, and indirect discrimination by identifying biases in apparently neutral procedures. These biases are harder to identify than unfair treatment justified by the expression of prejudices. Subtle discrimination is mainly detected as their disproportionate negative consequences on protected groups. The EEOC in the US defines an adverse impact in employment as "a substantially different rate of selection in hiring, promotion, or other employment decision which works to the disadvantage of members of a race, sex, or ethnic group." The EU law develops a similar approach in its definition of indirect discrimination (see Chap. 2), as the European Convention on Human Rights which retains that "a difference in treatment may take the form of disproportionately prejudicial effects of a general policy or measure which, though couched in neutral terms, discriminates against a group."

Thus, decisions, procedures, and selection schemes (in employment, housing, education, but also in the allocation of goods and services) have to be monitored to check the impartiality or neutrality of the process. Monitoring systems are frequently, but not exclusively, using statistics to detect under-representation of protected groups and biases in processes of selection or allocation of goods and services. It should be clear that the notion of fair representation is attached to those of statistical under-representation, which gives a paramount role of statistics in the identification of discrimination, the design of policies, their implementation, and their evaluation.

In order to be effective, equality programs in employment must follow these steps as part of their implementation: First, the definition and identification of members of protected groups. This is necessary to collect data, and especially statistics, on their proportion in all aspects of the employment process, such as in the applicant pools. Second, to collect data on the distribution of protected groups in different occupations in the firm, according to the level of qualification of the employees, wages, terminations, access to on the job-training, etc. Third, to compare these data to a statistical benchmark computed at different geographical levels and inside the firm itself to identify the potential gaps, which should then be corrected. Based on these statistical assessments, action plans are designed to reduce or suppress biases at the different steps of the employment relationship (hiring process, wage setting, and career advancement). In essence, equality programs combine the goals of improving the representation of protected groups with meritocratic criteria, since qualifications and skills are still the determining factors in the protected groups' representation.

7.2.4 Quantitative Targets and Quotas

Redressing the under-representation of protected groups can be achieved through quantitative objectives. The idea is to measure the evolution of the participation of protected groups to the organizations until they reach a threshold that has been established beforehand. These quantitative objectives can be mandatory, and in this case, one can speak of quotas to achieve, or an invitation to reach a target without specific sanctions if the organization fails to meet its objectives. When a quota is imposed, the organization (university, employer, landlord, parliament) must select a number or proportion of applicants with a specific characteristic (e.g., gender, ethnicity or race, disability, religion) to be incorporated in the program. An example can be given in political representation with reserved seats for women in India or legislated gender quota among candidates to political mandate in six EU countries, in employment for people with disability or in education for ethno-racial minorities in the US in the first phase of affirmative action (until 1973 in employment and 1978 in education). If the quota is not achieved, sanctions (generally financial penalties) against employers or universities might be enforced.

The legitimacy and efficiency of quotas have been extensively discussed in the US, especially during the 1980s with the disengagement from affirmative action by the administration under President Reagan. Although the available research suggests that quotas can be an effective tool, this instrument has often been poorly implemented and remained a contentious provision that is often criticized (Stryker

2001). As a policy tool, racial quotas have been discontinued in the US, but remain in some countries such as Brazil and Malaysia.

In opposition to quotas, most of the countries have adopted a more lenient approach by setting targets and goals that are still using quantitative tools but not in a mandatory way. For example, positive actions in the UK or equal employment opportunity policy in Canada are explicitly forbidding any quota. In these cases, the advantage given to members of protected groups does not appear as explicit as it is the case for preferential treatment.

One important condition for implementing these quantitative strategies is to be able to produce statistics broken down by ethnicity or race, or any kind of relevant category under protection. When it comes to ethnicity and race, the availability of such statistics is rather limited in most of the European countries, and thus limit the diffusion of these tools.

7.3   Promoting Diversity

Aside from public policies, there are initiatives undertaken directly by the business community. Although diversity management at its inception was a by-product of equal employment policies (Dobbin 2011), it has often been implemented by companies in countries where such policies have never been developed, especially in Europe (Wrench 2007). Indeed, the spread of diversity management seems to reflect the extension of multinational companies and the standardization of human resources processes. Diversity management tools include audits to identify biases in the organizational processes, mentoring programs, career guidance, diversity training, outreach activities toward underrepresented groups to diversify recruitment channels, etc.

The main idea behind these initiatives is that creating a diversity-friendly workplace by facilitating the recruitment, inclusion, promotion, and retention of "diverse employees" and managing properly this diverse workforce will help to increase productivity and give a market advantage to companies both in the domestic market – by reaching out to immigrants and their descendants as customers – and in markets abroad. Likewise, in the context of labor shortages, developing diversity management tools has become an important means for attracting and retaining staff. In addition, there may also be a value-added stemming from diversity itself because bringing together people with different backgrounds, experiences, and perspectives may increase the potential and the expertise of the working unit. Developing a diversity plan and targeting a fair representation of minority members in the workforce also have other benefits by helping to reduce the risks of litigations. The objective here is the reduction of the legal threat and the penalties resulting from legal cases. Further, employees may favor working environments that promote inclusion, respect, openness, collaboration, and equity. Finally, diversity management may involve benefits in terms of better publicity, and thus be used as a reputational tool by the firm. The European Commission has popularized the advantages of diversity in the economy under the heading of the business case for diversity (2005).

Diversity management has its roots in the US during the 1980s, during the peak of equal employment policies. A new class of "diversity managers" was created to implement actions against systemic discrimination rather than intentional discrimination. In 1980, diversity management was applied by less than 5% of a sample of 389 employers surveyed by Dobbin and Kelly, and almost 50% of them had implemented it by 1997 (Dobbin et al. 2007). In Europe, a survey conducted in 2005 found that 52% of companies did not develop any diversity initiatives, and only 21% had well-embedded policies and practices (European Commission 2005). The main motivations of these latter companies were (1) "commitment to equality and diversity as company values," (2) "access to new labor pools and high-quality employees," and (3) "economic effectiveness, competitiveness, and profitability. In contrast to the US, compliance with the law was not a major driver for these companies, which reflects that the antidiscrimination framework in Europe tends to be less pressuring. Interestingly, the survey showed also that only 31% of the companies implementing diversity initiatives were monitoring and reporting the results and impacts of their actions. In the remaining 69%, enhancing diversity was mainly an intention that could not be assessed.

Whereas equal employment policies comprise legally binding compliance to standards and codes of practices, fulfilling a diversity charter or acquiring a diversity label depends on voluntary initiatives from organizations. In contrast to the latter, however, these tools involve public or semi-public bodies that are at least proposing the tool and – in the case of labels – involve certifying participation and compliance.

A diversity charter is a document by which a company or a public institution commits itself to respect and promote diversity and equal opportunities at the workplace. More or less detailed provisions or targets can be stated in these charters. One of the first of its kind in Europe, the French diversity charter, was launched in October 2004 and has been signed by more than 3450 companies since then. This example has been replicated by almost all EU countries. The country-specific charters differ by their coverage and their scope, but the commitments are similar in their principles. Being voluntary, these charters do not entail specific monitoring to check if companies respect their commitments. As such, the charters testify that the companies show some concerns about promoting diversity, even if such a concern may not necessarily translate into concrete actions. Reviews of the actions implemented according to the charter are suggested, but in most cases, the audits focus on the design of the programs and not on their outcomes.

Diversity labels go one step further by delivering a certification based on an assessment of the measures taken and their implementation. An independent body is responsible for delivering the label, which is based on an audit of the companies. A diversity label was established in France in 2008 and is delivered by a commission made up of representatives of the national administration, the social partners, the National Organization of Human Resources Managers and experts. The label is delivered for 3 years; more than 260 companies have received it thus far. A similar diversity label is granted by the Brussels-Capital Region in Belgium. Some countries, such as Belgium, have also established specific diversity awards, rewarding good practices in this domain by employers.

Among the elements that can produce discrimination, notably with respect to the crucial first stage of the recruitment process, the formatting and contents of the CV of job applicants have been a major concern among equal opportunity policy makers and diversity managers. The recruitment process involves some kind of discretion from recruiters, and the more the room for discretion, the more stereotypes and prejudice might be activated. A concrete strategy to reduce the level of discretion in hiring procedures is to standardized job application documents in a way that only useful information about the applicants should be delivered. Building on the findings of correspondence test studies that clearly show that names and other signals of minority background foster negative selection (see Chaps. 4 and 5), the idea to promote blind or anonymous CVs has gained traction in France, Germany, and the UK. The advantage of anonymous CVs is to reduce the information that conveys signals related to discrimination, such as age, gender and ethnicity/race or nationality. The expectation is that applicants who will not be screened out at the first stage of the process will be able to demonstrate their capacities at the later stage and will eventually access higher opportunities for recruitment. A body of studies has tried to measure the outcomes of this measure in Germany (Krause et al. 2012), the Netherlands (Blommaert et al. 2014), France (Behaghel et al. 2015) and in Sweden (Aslund and Skans 2012). All of these studies but one (in France) found that ethnic minorities benefit from anonymity, but still encounter a harder selection at the stage of the job interview. The French study concluded that while women did benefit from anonymity, this was not the case for applicants with a minority background. One explanation for this unexpected finding, shared by Krause et al. (2012) in Germany, is that employers who favor diversity might advantage applicants with a migration background.

7.4   Assessing Antidiscrimination Policies

The complex schemes of monitoring and reporting attached to antidiscrimination laws and policies clearly run the risk of only being an attractive but purposeless platform if the operators do not fully commit to the program. Supervising the achievement of programs is, therefore, an inseparable element contributing to their efficiency. In most cases, compliance with monitoring is not guaranteed by sanctions or penalties, and participation in reporting may be far from effective.

In the Netherlands, the assessment of monitoring provided for by the 1994 *Wet bevordering evenredige arbeidskansen voor allochtonen* (Act on the Promotion of Proportional Labor market Participation of Allochtones; Wet BEAA) demonstrates that only 14% of employers fulfill all of the legal provisions, including the submission of a report on the situation of minorities within the company (Guiraudon et al. 2005). Less than 60% of these had applied for the obligatory registration of the ethnic origin of employees. The *Act for Stimulation of Labour Market Participation*, which replaced the Wet BEAA in 1998, clearly improved the level of participation, however: In 2001, 70% of employers prepared an annual report detailing the level of representation of ethnic minorities within their company and the measures taken to improve this over the following year. However, while the objectives set representation at 10%, the results reached their ceiling at 8.5%. Although employers with more than 35 people staff were legally obliged to register ethnicity and to submit reports every year, they could also refuse to comply without having to motivate their refusal. The decision to discontinue the SAMEN law in 2003 was partly justified by the lack of participation of employers in the scheme (Guiraudon et al. 2005).

In the UK, the assessment of equality policies is incorporated into the design of the equality programs themselves. Under the Race Relation Act of 2000 (amended), the duties are stricter for public authorities than for private employers. A 1998 survey on the working conditions within companies (Workplace Employee Relations Survey, WERS), which was analyzed in 2003, showed that equality programs are applied within two thirds of companies, 97% of public companies and 57% from the private sector. The programs are implemented more often in companies that have a higher representation of "minorities" (women, ethnic minorities, and disabled people). Among the various actions provided for by the equality programs, the monitoring of employees' ethnic and racial origin is only carried out by 30% of companies. This disappointing level of monitoring also applies to companies from the public sector, where only 48% of companies have implemented it.

A review by Dex and Purdam (2005) did not find significant improvements after the amendment of the Race Relation Act in UK in 2000: the Commission for Racial Equality found in 2003 that just over a third of organizations were responding to the duties, though most of the public organizations had produced a race equality scheme or policy. In the private sector, a 2003 survey with 500 UK directors identified similar gaps between policies aiming at promoting equal opportunities and the implementation of monitoring system: only 38% of organizations had collected information on the number of employees by ethnic group, and 22% got this information by job positions. In their review of the monitoring practices of ten employers in UK, Dex and Purdam (2005) revealed that although all the employers were collecting data for equal opportunities monitoring purposes, only a few were able to compile these data in tables with standardized categories matching the codes of practice of the Commission for Racial Equality, and hardly any of them were analyzing the data produced (Dex and Purdam 2005, 16–18).

Beyond the assessments of a system's performance, which is an important condition in assessing its results, a key question remains unanswered: Do the schemes succeed in reducing the consequences of discrimination, easing prejudice, and improving the position of the protected groups? Few programs provide appraisals linking the implementation of initiatives with the improvement of the situation of the protected groups. The Employment Equity Act Annual Reports in Canada, however, are notable exceptions as they provide this type of appraisal. A representation index by group is calculated for each company and business sector. Its variation provides an indication of the impact of the programs. In 2010, the representation of aboriginals, women, and visible minorities had improved, both quantitatively and qualitatively. On the other hand, this remained poor for disabled people. The representation index (the rate of availability relating to the size of a group within the labor force) is established at 95.9 for women, 80.7 for natives and 77.5 for visible minorities but only 46.9 for disabled people.

In the US, a great deal of research has been conducted to assess the impact of affirmative action on employment and education for minorities and women. Holzer and Neumark (2000) demonstrate that the organizations that have adopted the affirmative action programs have seen a clear improvement in the representation of minorities and women in relation to those who did not. However, women, and especially white women, have benefited more from these policies than racial minorities. These findings have been renewed by the evaluation of the outcomes of diversity programs conducted by Dobbin and Kalev (2016). In an assessment of the employment practices and workforce reviews of more than 800 companies in the US from 1971 to 2002, they conclude that mandatory diversity training was producing poor return while programs strengthening managerial responsibility and accountability with respect to equality tended to be particularly effective.

7.5   Conclusion

This chapter has reviewed how policies can address discrimination, with the different frames and tools that have been adopted. The first stage of these policies is to raise awareness and disseminate concepts and definitions of discrimination in legal action. The second and more effective stage aims at monitoring decision-making processes and selection practices to promote equal treatment beyond formal principles. Proactive policies can be called positive action or affirmative action: in all cases, they rely on the existence of statistics broken down by ethnicity, race, or equivalent characteristics to uncover unfair treatment and disadvantage faced by minorities. The lack of such statistics in schools, workplaces, housing, or health systems makes it complicated, if not impossible, to implement most of the schemes of positive action policies. This explains why most European countries fail to develop effective policies against ethnic and racial discrimination, in stark contrast with gender equality programs.

Because antidiscrimination policies address structural inequalities rooted in historical systems of domination, it would be very optimistic to think that they could redress wrongs done by long established and renewed prejudices. For this reason, they have to be judged in the long run. Not only do they need time to effectively tackle discrimination, but their legitimacy is always fragile. If public opinion accepts the implementation of policies and actions targeting minorities when responsibilities of the state are obvious, such support declines dramatically when blatant racism and racial gaps tend to diminish. Opposition to race-based affirmative action or positive action has increased in countries that have pioneered such policies, such as the US. This reminds us that fighting discrimination is not a zero-sum game: when losers improve their position, former winners tend to regret their privileges.

References

Allouch, A., & Buisson-Fenet, H. (2009). The minor roads to excellence: Positive action, outreach policies, and the new positioning of elite high schools in France and England. *International Studies in Sociology of Education, 19*(3–4), 229–244. https://doi.org/10.1080/09620210903424592.

Aslund, O., & Skans, O. N. (2012). Do anonymous job application procedures level the playing field? *Industrial and Labor Relations Review, 65*(1), 82–107.

Behaghel, L., Crépon, B., & Le Barbanchon, T. (2015). Unintended effects of anonymous Résumés. *American Economic Journal: Applied Economics, 7*(3), 1–27. https://doi.org/10.1257/app.20140185.

Blommaert, L., Coenders, M., & van Tubergen, F. (2014). Discrimination of Arabic-named applicants in the Netherlands: An internet-based field experiment examining different phases in online recruitment procedures. *Social Forces, 92*(3), 957–982.

de Witte, B. (2010). From a 'common principle of equality' to 'European antidiscrimination law. *American Behavioral Scientist, 53*(12), 1715–1730. https://doi.org/10.1177/0002764210368093.

Dex, S., & Purdam, K. (2005). *Equal opportunities and recruitment: How census data can help employers to assess their practices.* York: Joseph Rowntree Foundation, University of Manchester.

Dobbin, F. (2011). *Inventing equal opportunity.* Princeton: Princeton University Press.

Dobbin, F., & Kalev, A. (2016). Why diversity programs fail. *Harvard Business Review, 94*(7), 52–60.

Dobbin, F., Kalev, A., & Kelly, E. (2007). Diversity Management in Corporate America. *Contexts, 6*(4), 21–28. https://doi.org/10.1525/ctx.2007.6.4.21.

European Commission. (2005). *The business case for diversity: Good practices in the workplace.* Brussels: European Commission.

FRA. (2012). *Access to justice in cases of discrimination in the EU – Steps to further equality.* Vienna: FRA – European Union Agency for Fundamental Rights.

Fredman, S. (2016). Substantive equality revisited. *International Journal of Constitutional Law, 14*(3), 712–738. https://doi.org/10.1093/icon/mow043.

Guiraudon, V., Phalet, K., & Ter Wal, J. (2005). Monitoring ethnic minorities in the Netherlands. *International Social Science Journal, 57*(183), 75–87. https://doi.org/10.1111/j.0020-8701.2005.00532.x.

Holzer, H. J., & Neumark, D. (2000). Assessing affirmative action. *Journal of Economic Literature, XXXVIII,* 483–568. https://doi.org/10.1257/jel.38.3.483.

Krause, A., Rinne, U., & Zimmermann, K. (2012). Anonymous job applications in Europe. *IZA Journal of European Labor Studies, 1,* 5. https://doi.org/10.1186/2193-9012-1-5.

McCrudden, C. (1986). Rethinking positive action. *Industrial Law Journal, 15*(1), 219–243. https://doi.org/10.1093/ilj/15.1.219.

Sabbagh, D. (2011). Affirmative action: The U.S. experience in comparative perspective. *Daedalus, 140*(2), 109–120. https://doi.org/10.1162/DAED_a_00081.

Simon, P. (2005). The measurement of racial discrimination: The policy use of statistics. *International Journal of Social Science, 57*(183), 9–25. https://doi.org/10.1111/j.0020-8701.2005.00528.x.

Stryker, R. (2001). Disparate impact and the quota debates: Law, labor market sociology, and equal employment policies. *The Sociological Quarterly, 42*(1), 13–46. https://doi.org/10.1111/j.1533-8525.2001.tb02373.x.

Wrench, J. (2007). *Diversity management and discrimination: Immigrants and ethnic minorities in the EU.* Aldershot: Ashgate.

Chapter 8
Conclusion

This book has provided an overview of the current field of discrimination research, emphasizing how race, ethnicity and minority status shape current opportunities in Europe. It has outlined key concepts, theories, and methods; suggested how discrimination plays out differently in different social domains and how experiences of discrimination impact individuals and groups; and it has provided a brief synthesis of the policies developed to combatting discrimination.

Since its inception as a research field in the US in the 1950s, the study of discrimination has flourished over the last 20–30 years in Europe. This is no coincidence. European countries have, in this time period, gradually turned multicultural and multireligious, where a continuous inflow of immigrants from all over the world, alongside the coming of age of their descendants, has triggered an unprecedented level of migration-related diversity. Today, most European countries are characterized by high levels of ethno-racial inequality, where disparities between groups in education, work, housing, and health are striking. Decades of research have made evident that widespread discrimination plays a role in creating these inequalities, raising the question of whether the previously dominant conceptual frame of integration is insufficient or even inadequate to account for the socio-structural position of ethno-racial minorities over time.

8.1 Pervasive, Perpetuating, and Persistent

As shown by the last Eurobarometer survey on discrimination (European Commission 2019), the awareness of ethnic discrimination is present, as it is perceived as widespread by 59% of respondents in Europe. However, this awareness does not suggest that proactive antidiscrimination policies find large support, nor that prejudices against ethnic, racial, and religious minorities have diminished. Rather, the findings of the impressive breadth of research reveal a worrying picture of enduring discrimination in immigrant-receiving societies across space and time,

© The Author(s) 2021
R. Fibbi et al., *Migration and Discrimination*, IMISCOE Research Series,
https://doi.org/10.1007/978-3-030-67281-2_8

suggesting the contour of troubling "three P's" in contemporary European societies: discrimination appears to be pervasive, perpetuating, and persistent.

8.1.1   Pervasive Presence

First of all, meta-analyses have documented that immigrant-origin groups face significant discrimination in access to employment in nine countries in Europe and North America (Quillian et al. 2019), a well as in the broader OECD area (Zschirnt and Ruedin 2016). Yet the level of discrimination seems to vary considerably across national contexts: In some countries, native-majority job applicants receive close to twice the callbacks of minority applicants, while in others, natives receive about 25% more (Quillian et al. 2019). This cross-national variation suggests that the institutional contexts surrounding discriminatory actions matter.

8.1.2   Perpetuating Configuration

In contrast to predictions in integration and assimilation theories, the level of discrimination facing immigrants and their descendants do not seem to differ substantially. This suggests that ethnicity, and presumably religion, are driving factors for discrimination (Heath and Cheung 2007; Carlsson 2010; Zschirnt and Ruedin 2016; Di Stasio et al. 2019). Moreover, abundant evidence from a range of different studies shows the existence of clear ethnic hierarchies, where European-origin groups experience significantly less discrimination than non-European origin groups. Such group differences in the level of discrimination are documented directly, by the use of field experiments, (Quillian et al. 2019), as well as indirectly, by the use of the residual method (e.g., Heath et al. 2008; Heath and Brinbaum 2014) and various studies of experiences of discrimination (e.g., Beauchemin et al. 2018; Beigang et al. 2017; Andriessen et al. 2014). In sum, these studies suggest that a growing process of racialization is currently taking place in Europe.

8.1.3   Persistent Pattern

A major concern arises from the fact that, in spite of the implementation of antidiscrimination measures, levels of hiring discrimination in the US and the UK remain largely unchanged over time (Quillian et al. 2017; Heath and Di Stasio 2019). It is not clear whether the same is true for other European countries, yet the adoption of antidiscrimination legislation in Europe in the 2000s does not appear to have had an impact on the extent of discrimination (Zschirnt and Ruedin 2016). In many countries, measures to address discrimination have been adopted. Systematic monitoring of their implementation and of the effectiveness of single measures in various contexts could stimulate a collective learning process aimed at reaching beyond formal also effective equality.

8.2 Discrimination and Integration Revisited

The three P's raise fundamental questions about the long-term prospects of integration, as has been the dominant frame of analyses in the field of migration studies for decades. Of course, integration may occur despite persistent discrimination, as evident in the research on the so-called "integration paradox" (e.g., Schaeffer 2018; Steinmann 2018). Yet, we need to acknowledge that ethnic and racial discrimination is part of the current European reality, despite decades of legal efforts to eliminate the problem. How this affects the life chances and identity of Europe's ethno-racial minority groups, and whether it obscures the prospects of a long-term "mainstream expansion" (cf., Alba and Yrizar Barbosa 2016), are among the most pressing questions of today.

Although theories of integration and discrimination do not necessarily clash, significant contradictions arise when it comes to policies. Where antidiscrimination policies aim at adapting and transforming the structures of societies (institutions, laws, policies, procedures, practices, and representations) to make them fair and accessible to immigrants and minorities, integration policies mainly aim at empowering immigrants and their children by enhancing their human and social capital. Clearly, integration policies are not sufficient for addressing the persistence of discrimination. Much more work is needed to understand what diversity or antidiscrimination policies work in limiting bias and reducing discrimination.

8.3 Avenues for Future Research

The many advancements of discrimination research over the past decades, combined with the growing concern of the consequences of discrimination at both the individual, group, and societal levels, point out a range of future research prospects. Experimental methods have been the key approach to measure the prevalence of discrimination, yet the use of this methodology in Europe has not yet been able to disentangle the effects of racial appearance and religious beliefs on opportunities in labor or housing markets. Due to problems of comparability across research designs, experimental studies of discrimination also have a long way to go in investigating how particularities of institutional contexts shape the level of discrimination.

Apart from quantitative and experimental studies that provide estimates of the prevalence of discrimination in societies committed to equality of opportunity, many qualitative studies have looked closer into the reactions among those exposed to unfair treatment, blatant racism, and micro-aggressions in everyday life. Victims of discrimination are not without agency to react and counter unfair treatment, even though they might prefer to ignore their negative experiences rather than speak against them. Clearly, reacting to discrimination is preconditioned by a consciousness of its existence. The function of research on discrimination is also to create the conditions for this consciousness to rise among minority groups, public authorities, and civil society. More research is needed to fully understand the costs and consequences of discrimination and how experiences of discrimination shape life chances, identity, and potential withdrawal from mainstream society.

Importantly, studying ethnic and racial discrimination requires having access to reliable and comparable data describing population groups that are categorized in relevant categories (i.e., related to ethnicity and race). Statistics in Europe are mainly based on nationality and place of birth, and in only a handful of countries is the same information available about the parents of domestic-born minorities (the second and later generations). These categories only partly describe groups and individuals that are facing ethnic and racial discrimination. The choice to deem ethnic and racial categories as irrelevant and even dangerous has its historical rationale, but the lack of data makes it complicated to map out and understand the consequences of the ongoing process of racialization in European societies (Simon 2017). The lack of appropriate data not only jeopardizes a detailed knowledge of discrimination processes, but it prevents the implementation of monitoring of procedures and practices meant to enhance diversity in domains such as education, work, and health and thus entails a severe limitation in the development of effective antidiscrimination policies. How to establish categories that enable researchers to identify the barriers facing ethno-racial minorities that are at present not detectable in national statistics will be a question of major importance in the years to come.

Even if we have focused on ethnic and racial discrimination in this book, multiple grounds of discrimination are often present in the experience of unfair treatment. Intersectionality is a conceptual framework that offers heuristic perspectives for research on discrimination, and it should be developed beyond the usual articulation between gender and race or class and ethnicity. The increase of religious discrimination against Muslims in Europe – a phenomenon often referred to as Islamophobia – is changing the conceptual frames of ethnic and racial studies (Taras 2012). As shown by recent research in Europe, prejudices against Muslims are widespread (EUMC 2006; Strabac and Listhaug 2008; FRA 2017), fostering what has been called a "racialization of religion" (Meer 2014). Whether and how religion is replacing ethnicity or race as a marker of identity, and hence as the basis of discrimination, should receive more attention in future studies.

References

Alba, R., & Yrizar Barbosa, G. (2016). Room at the top? Minority mobility and the transition to demographic diversity in the USA. *Ethnic and Racial Studies, 39*(6), 917–938. https://doi.org/1 0.1080/01419870.2015.1081966.

Andriessen, I., Fernee, H., & Wittebrood, K. (2014). *Perceived discrimination in the Netherlands.* Den Haag: Netherlands Institute for Social Research (SCP).

Beauchemin, C., Hamel, C., & Simon, P. (Eds.). (2018). *Trajectories and origins: Survey on the diversity of the French population* (INED population studies 8). Cham: Springer.

Beigang, S., Fetz, K., Kalkum, D., & Otto, M. (2017). *Diskriminierungserfahrungen in Deutschland: Ergebnisse einer Repräsentativ- und einer Betroffenenbefragung.* Antidiskriminierungsstelle des Bundes. Baden-Baden: Nomos.

Carlsson, M. (2010). Experimental evidence of discrimination in the hiring of first- and second-generation immigrants. *Labour, 24*(3), 263–278. https://doi.org/10.1111/j.1467-9914.2010. 00482.x.

Di Stasio, V., Lancee, B., Veit, S., & Yemane, R. (2019). Muslim by default or religious discrimination? Results from a cross-national field experiment on hiring discrimination. *Journal of Ethnic and Migration Studies.* https://doi.org/10.1080/1369183X.2019.1622826.

European Commission. (2019). *Discrimination in the EU* (Special Eurobarometer 493). Brussels: European Commission.

European Monitoring Centre on racism and xenophobia (EUMC). (2006). *Muslims in the European Union: Discrimination and Islamophobia.* European Monitoring Centre on Racism and Islamophobia.

FRA. (2017). *Second European Union minorities and discrimination survey: Muslims – Selected findings.* Luxembourg: Publications Office of the European Union.

Heath, A., & Brinbaum, Y. (Eds.). (2014). *Unequal attainments. Ethnic educational inequalities in ten Western countries.* Oxford: Oxford University Press.

Heath, A. F., & Cheung, S. Y. (Eds.). (2007). *Unequal chances: Ethnic minorities in Western labour markets.* Oxford: British Academy/Oxford University Press.

Heath, A., & Di Stasio, V. (2019). Racial discrimination in Britain, 1969–2017: A meta-analysis of field experiments on racial discrimination in the British labour market. *British Journal of Sociology.* https://doi.org/10.1111/1468-4446.12676.

Heath, A. F., Rothon, C., & Kilpi, E. (2008). The second generation in Western Europe: Education, unemployment, and occupational attainment. *Annual Review of Sociology, 34,* 211–235. https://doi.org/10.1146/annurev.soc.34.040507.134728.

Meer, N. (Ed.). (2014). *Racialization and religion: Race, culture, and difference in the study of antisemitism and Islamophobia.* London: Routledge.

Quillian, L., Hexel, O., Pager, D., & Midtbøen, A. H. (2017). Meta-analysis of field experiments shows no change in racial discrimination in hiring over time. *Proceedings of the National Academy of the Sciences in the United States, 114*(41), 10870–10875. https://doi.org/10.1073/ pnas.1706255114.

Quillian, L., Heath, A., Pager, D., Midtbøen, A. H., Fleischmann, F., & Hexel, O. (2019). Do some countries discriminate more than others? Evidence from 97 field experiments of racial discrimination in hiring. *Sociological Science, 6,* 467–496. https://doi.org/10.15195/v6.a18.

Schaeffer, M. (2018). Social mobility and perceived discrimination: Adding an intergenerational perspective. *European Sociological Review, 35*(1), 65–80. https://doi.org/10.1093/esr/jcy042.

Simon, P. (2017). The failure of the importation of ethno-racial statistics in Europe: Debates and controversies. *Ethnic and Racial Studies, 40*(13), 2326–2332. https://doi.org/10.1080/0141987 0.2017.1344278.

Steinmann, J.-P. (2018). The paradox of integration: Why do higher educated new immigrants perceive more discrimination in Germany? *Journal of Ethnic and Migration Studies,* 1–24. https:// doi.org/10.1080/1369183X.2018.1480359.

Strabac, Z., & Listhaug, O. (2008). Anti-Muslim prejudice in Europe: A multilevel analysis of survey data from 30 countries. *Social Science Research, 37*(1), 268–286. https://doi. org/10.1016/j.ssresearch.2007.02.004.

Taras, R. (2012). *Xenophobia and Islamophobia in Europe*. Edinburg: Edinburgh University Press.

Zschirnt, E., & Ruedin, D. (2016). Ethnic discrimination in hiring decisions: A meta-analysis of correspondence tests 1990–2015. *Journal of Ethnic & Migration Studies, 42*(7), 1115–1134. https://doi.org/10.1080/1369183X.2015.1133279.